The Principal

A-8531

The odyssey of a "mountain boy" from the
Carpathian Mountains of Eastern Europe, via the
Nazi concentration camps, to become the principal of
a prestigious parochial school in the Rocky Mountains
of the United States of America.

Rabbi Israel Rosenfeld

KODESH PRESS

Cover art by Faith Williams.
Additional Formatting by Kodesh Press.

Published & Distributed by
Kodesh Press L.L.C.
New York, NY
www.KodeshPress.com
KodeshPress@gmail.com
(914) 819-3611

DEDICATION

This volume is dedicated to
the loving memory of my mother,

חנה (חנטשי) בת ר' עזרא הלוי, ע"ה
Chana (Chantshi) Rosenfeld

whose wisdom, dedication, and love gave meaning and
substance to our survival. Her life was not easy, but
her rewards were great. She never forgot Auschwitz or
her great loses. She left this world at a ripe old age, on
November 2, 1995, with great *nachas* and joy from what
G-d had returned to her.

May her loving memory be a constant beacon to all of us
who loved her and miss her so very much.

ת.נ.צ.ב.ה.

Denver, Colorado
August 2014

ACKNOWLEDGEMENTS

I deeply appreciate the efforts of my former
student and friends for their efforts in initiating this project:

Scott Friedman,
Amichai Ungar,
and Dr. Terry Samuel

.

CONTENTS

INTRODUCTION

This true story is a heavily redacted version of my original autobiography (*My Life*) since that version contains information that would be of interest only to my immediate family.

The passage of time, since the horrors of the Holocaust, close to seventy years now, has probably taken its toll on the sharp images that once tormented my memories and made "normal" life unthinkable. I am very worried now that if I procrastinate any further it will become impossible to describe not only the tortures of the Holocaust and their consequences, but also the fifteen years of my very unique childhood preceding it, as well as what life was like after it.

I can't say that I find this task to be pleasurable by any means. I see it as fulfilling a responsibility and an obligation that all of us who came through the "Gates of Hell" owe to those martyred souls who can no longer tell their own stories.

Since the end of the Second World War, I have painstakingly avoided reading any materials or watching any movies or T.V. programs that deal with the Holocaust and its aftermath. I never visited the exhibits at Yad Vashem in Jerusalem, nor the Holocaust Museum in Washington, in order not to clutter up my own memories of those horrific events. In 1954, on my very first visit to Israel, I attempted to visit Martef HaShoah (the Holocaust Cellar) on Mount Zion. The trauma that I experienced there, a total and complete breakdown, convinced me that I am not strong enough, and probably never will be, to relive any part of those terrible events.

I also strongly believe that we can't speak of "the Holocaust," as if it were the same, uniform event felt and experienced equally by everyone involved. In reality there were six million, and many more, individual Holocausts felt differently by each victim, martyr, or survivor, depending on his or her own emotional, social, and educational backgrounds and maturity. We can't, therefore, borrow from others' accounts and adopt them as our own. I am convinced that I will forget many events and details that might be important and include some details that may be totally frivolous. However, what I do manage to relate, will be my own, untainted recollections of my life, the way that only I remember them (even if somewhat hazily).

My life has certainly been "interesting" to say the least. My account is of the odyssey of a boy from the Carpathian Mountains who retired as the principal and administrator of a very prestigious private school in the Rocky Mountains of Colorado after 25 years of service, and an additional three years as principal and administrator of another such school in Hartford, Connecticut. This journey and the transformation were not easy, nor smooth. My path took many twisted turns and unimaginable obstacles to move from one mountain range to the other. It was a journey that lasted over sixty years and spanned over several thousand miles. I am not even certain that this "metamorphosis" is yet complete.

In order to fully grasp the magnitude and the background of my own, private Holocaust, and of what life held for me afterward, it is necessary, I feel, to paint as full a picture as possible of my formative years and of the social and cultural milieu of those experiences.

There will, obviously, appear some gaps in the narrative due to the fact that I am editing my story to leave out some confidential materials as well as some details that would not be interesting to the casual reader.

The Accident

I sit there, trembling uncontrollably. The ambulance ride with x to the emergency room, with her arm spouting blood soaking through the towels packed with ice, did not allow me even a moment's respite to contemplate what had happened and to formulate in my mind a cohesive report to give her parents when they arrive at the hospital.

After x is wheeled into the operating room, and I have to remain outside, by myself, a familiar feeling of panic slowly begins to take over. How will I face those parents? Will they hold me personally responsible? After all, they are Holocaust survivors, too, just like me, and I know how over-protective we tend to be about our children. In addition, we also happen to be neighbors, and our children play together all the time.

As has become my habit ever since I became the principal of the Academy, in times of stress, I revert to self-doubt about my *chutzpah* to accept such a position of responsibility. By what right do I, a refugee kid from a little *shtetl* in Eastern Europe, dare to assume such a highly respected, prestigious position? Surely, it is just a matter of time before I will stumble, and reveal for all to see my ineptness. Sooner or later, I'll be exposed as a fraud.... And now it is finally happening!

Just a short time has elapsed since I drove up to the Academy, returning from an important meeting. My heart began pounding wildly when I saw the ambulance parked near the kitchen entrance in the school yard. Now what?!, I'd thought.... Who did what to whom? Who got hurt? Could it have been avoided had I not left the building while the children were there? Did I act as a "responsible adult" as the legal books state that every adult in charge of protecting the wellbeing of children must act? The principal is also responsible, by law, to provide "a safe and secure environment" for his students. There were close to 300 of them at the school. I had no assistant principal to share any of the responsibilities with me.

Flying down the stairs to the kitchen level, I burst into the kitchen. I have to hold on to something before my knees completely buckle. The scene unfolding is horrendous. The blood almost completely covers a section of the cement floor. On one table x is lying, white as a ghost. The paramedics are trying to stop the bleeding of her arm which is gashed on the inside almost the entire length, all the blood vessels severed. They apply ice, pressure bandages, and tourniquets. The blood comes rushing through the bandages and the towels. I think I might faint.

When the paramedics stabilize the bleeding, they wheel her into the waiting ambulance. I insist on riding along with her. She is only an adolescent and would surely be frightened without a familiar face around her for reassurance. I leave word with one of the secretaries to call her parents to meet us at the hospital, and to make an announcement over the intercom that x will be alright, and to tell the teachers, discreetly, not to take children downstairs until the custodian has a chance to clean up.

During the ride to the hospital I am filled in by the medics on the details, which I had only heard in general terms at the scene.

Our Academy is housed in a brand new, somewhat modernistic, school building. It is very beautiful but not very practical or utilitarian for the intended purpose. The staff used to joke about the probability that the architect who designed it probably never designed a school building before, and it is quite possible that he never attended one either.

The lower level serves as an all-purpose lunchroom, assembly hall, and gymnasium; to make it look better and have some natural day light come in, the architect had put along one wall several full-length glass windows, from ceiling to floor. It looked very nice. However, nobody contemplated the tragedy waiting to happen when a child would run full speed after a runaway ball during gym class. Neither the cement walls nor the window panes had any padding or protecting rails.

This day, during gym class, *x*, in hot pursuit after a ball, smashed into one of the windows. The shattered glass cut the length of her arm. By a sheer miracle, the large sections of the falling, broken glass did not cut her neck too.

I feel cold sweat covering me. I am scared. While waiting for word from the OR physician and for her parents to arrive, my mind is racing and conjuring up bits and pieces from my past that haunt me whenever I am under great pressure. My background, it seems to me during these times of deep reflection, did indeed prepare me for these kinds of situations.

My history was certainly unique and unusual. I had survived great tragedies in my life before, and I know that I will also come out of this experience intact.

MEIN SHTETLE—CHUST

Chust or Chist or Huszt or Xycm is a small town in the Maramorosh Region that was divided between Hungary and Rumania (and later on, between Rumania and Czechoslovakia). To find it on a map, you will need a good magnifying glass. In what country or state to look for it will depend on the vintage of the map itself. If it was printed before the year 1918 you would look for it in the Austro-Hungarian Empire. If the map was printed between the years 1918 and 1939, you would find it at the eastern end of Czechoslovakia. On a map printed between 1939 and 1945 you it would be somewhere in the north-eastern part of Hungary. If, however, you should be fortunate enough to get hold of a rare map of the Independent Republic of Western Ukraine, printed sometime in March 1939, look for its capital city of Chust (or Xycm). If you study a map issued between 1945 and 1946, you should try to find it once again in Eastern Czechoslovakia. Between 1946 and today, you may be able to locate it at the Western edge of the Soviet Union (as the Zakarpatska Ukraina Oblast). I recall that during all public celebrations and in school assemblies, we got tired from standing at attention while all three national anthems, Czech, Slovak, and Ruthenia, were played by the band or sung by us. If all of this is somewhat confusing to you now, think of how utterly frustrating it was for us growing up under different states, flags, languages, schools, and national loyalties! No wonder we have difficulties in filling out questionnaires or forms where the simple question asks for your "previous nationality." Who knows what exact era they are interested in?

Only two references to Chust have never changed. It always was and will always remain one of the "big cities" in the Carpathian

Mountains of Eastern Europe. And it is also my place of birth and the site of my innocent, formative years. *Mein shtetle* (my little town)—Chust!

Chust may have changed owners and occupiers many times in history, but in reality it remained, more or less a sleepy little township of about 26,000 inhabitants. The setting is beautiful and even idyllic. It is surrounded on all sides by green mountains, huge forests, luscious meadows, and orchards. In the middle of the town there is a cone-shaped mountain called the Schlossbarg on account of the remaining ruins of an ancient castle (*schloss*) that adorns the top of the "pyramid." It is also blessed with an abundance of water. If my memory serves me right, there were four rivers in and around Chust, the largest being the Tissa or Tass. Then there were the Rika, the Nagyag, and the Husztviz, which lends its name to the city, even though it was seldom more awesome than a little creek that usually contained no more water than what the washer women needed to rinse the laundry. However, it became a raging and powerful menace in the spring time when the frozen river melted and huge chunks of ice formed a dam around the pylons of the wooden bridge and all the children spent their spare time watching and waiting with bated breath to see the bridge collapse and the little, mighty creek overflow its banks and flood a large area on both sides. The winters were very harsh. It snowed non-stop from October through March. The snow sometimes piled up as high as the windows. It was mercilessly cold and most children were coughing all winter long. In the winter months, horse-drawn sleds were the only means of transportation besides walking. Around March we had a great deal of fun chopping up with pickaxes the very thick layers of ice in our courtyard.

Most households, but definitely not all, had electricity. My grandmother's house had no electricity; neither did many of my friends' and neighbors' homes. Indoor plumbing or running water was seldom heard of and even more rarely actually seen in town. I, personally, had seen the wondrous "magic" of indoor plumbing for the first time in my life at about the age of 12 while visiting the Chief Rabbi's newly refurbished house. I had a very hard time understanding how people can relieve themselves inside the house rather than go to the outhouse for such an unpleasant activity. We did! We also had to go with buckets in hands, every few hours as needed, summer and winter, way back to the end of the courtyard (perhaps 200 yards or more) to draw fresh water for drinking, cooking, and washing, from the well. (Later on a hand pump was added, which seldom worked.) Perhaps ten percent or less of all the homes had indoor plumbing, and perhaps seventy-five percent had electricity.

The lack of indoor plumbing curtailed the extent of personal grooming and hygiene. During the week, most people washed their hands and faces in the morning in a "laver" basin, which was then poured out into the courtyard. Once a week, Thursday evenings, children would be bathed and scrubbed clean in a large wooden or metal trough with water heated up on the stove. Grown-ups and older children went to the *mikvah* frequently; some did so every morning. The "big *mikvah*" was usually filthy, including the water in it. It was a public bathhouse, where people came and scrubbed themselves in the same standing water that was not changed, filtered, or chemically treated perhaps for weeks, if ever. For most Hasidic men and women, it was also a purifying ritual bath. How they prevented outbreaks of contagious diseases is a mystery to me. This *mikvah* served thousands of people per week and was the poor man's place to get clean at least once a week before Shabbat. You can't imagine the thick filth, grime, and hair that floated on the water's surface, nor the assault to the nostrils from its foul smell.

For those who could afford it, next door was the "small *mikvah*." This was a completely different world. This place was always spotless and the water consistently clean and crystal clear. You could actually see the white ceramic tiles at the bottom. No one was allowed in the water before taking a hot shower with soap in one of the many private rooms. We were lucky. The man in charge of the *mikvah*, Kalman der bader, who stood there and collected the different fees for the use of the *mikvah*, was also our landlord and always permitted us to enter into the small one for the price of the big, filthy one for the common folks. How the non-Jewish townsfolk cleansed themselves also remains a mystery to me.

The lack of indoor plumbing also created a great problem and a real hardship for the homemakers, not so much with the cooking as with the laundry. Water had to be heated up on the stove and the laundry was hand washed in the wooden trough and on a washing board. This was a weekly chore and not too complicated. However, in the springtime a major ritual took place in town. It was referred to in Hungarian as *Nagy Moshash* – The Great Wash Day.

It is quite impossible to even imagine the hardship of living in a house lacking indoor plumbing. Can you imagine yourself in the middle of a sub-zero winter night urgently needing to use the toilet? Father had to be woken up, get dressed, light a candle or a lantern, walk with us outside, and stand guard by the latrines. The pain of an occasional splinter from the wooden seats was never pleasant.

Most streets were not paved at all and would turn into solid mud whenever it rained or when the snow melted. Some streets were paved with cobblestones. The main streets, however, were broad and paved with asphalt.

Many of the houses had no wooden floors, just pressed dirt. Some even had makeshift thatched roofs. The majority were small, one-family cottages, usually with several houses grouped in one, large, fenced-in *hoif* (courtyard). We lived with five other families in one courtyard. Heating was provided by wood-burning stoves that also were used for cooking and baking. The *Holtzplatz* was a very busy open marketplace, where the villagers brought in huge loads of uncut logs for sale by the wagon-full, to be cut up by the buyers into firewood. Transportation was mainly provided by horse-drawn wagons and *fiakers*. There was only one taxi in town available for special occasions. There was also a rickety old bus that shuttled people from the center of town to the main railroad station (there was also an auxiliary, much smaller, station, but not all trains stopped there). The town also had one gas pump. It was a contraption with two large upside-down bottles on top of it. The owner, Mr. Haber, would pump the handle back and forth until one bottle filled up, and while that first one emptied out into the vehicle, the other one filled up until the vehicle was full. We, the children, were fascinated by this machine and would stand and watch the tedious process whenever the occasional car or bus would pull up to the pump. There was no "station" there, just the one, lonesome, monolith-like pump.

There were two hotels in town, the Central and the Corona. I have no idea till this day who actually needed or made use of these fancy hotels. They were really very fine, two-floor buildings. They had non-kosher restaurants. The main floors of both housed very nice stores and shops. There were also a couple of inns for out-of-town visitors who also cared to have kosher food. There were a few restaurants and "bodegas" (something like a cross between a fast food eatery, delicatessen store, candy and fancy fruits store). Some displayed in their show-windows huge smoked goose livers and *griven*—melted down and deep-fried skin of geese and chickens.

There was also a very large and important military base at the edge of town, since Chust was the largest city guarding the mountain passes against invaders from the east. Because of this, we also had a very large contingent of customs officers who patrolled the mountain passes against smugglers of goods across the borders that lay only a few dozen miles to the east. The local constabulary was usually augmented by federal or state police hunting down the bandits and highwaymen who plundered and murdered travelers and smugglers alike. Two of these robbers, Nikolai and Shuhai, became legendary figures whose very names terrorized everyone until they were finally caught. They were publicly executed in the prison yard by hanging. Many stout-hearted people went to watch that curious event. However, most of my friends and their parents did not. All I remember of Nikolai and Shuhai were the fascinating legends and folk stories that were spun by people who claimed to have had actual encounters with these bandits. We lived in awe of them and wondered when and if they would ever descend from their mountain hideouts to rob and attack us. I also recall seeing a very large man strolling down the main street; we were told that he was the executioner brought to town by the authorities for that special occasion.

The inhabitants of Chust and of the rest of "Ruthenia" were a polyglot of national and ethnic groups. The majority belonged to a pseudo-Ukrainian sub-group commonly referred to as "Ruthenians" (in Yiddish we referred to them as *Rusnyaken*). They were by far the majority of the approximately 26,000 citizens in town. There were also about six or seven thousand Jewish inhabitants. Hungarians, Gypsies, Czechs, Schwabs (ethnic Germans), Bulgars, etc., completed the roster.

There were no industries, light or heavy, in the entire region. The largest factory in town was Dunkel's furniture factory that probably employed several dozen workers. The Segal family owned a combination of a *talis*, hat, and sweater factory that also employed a few dozen people. Shopkeepers, tradesmen, and other self-employed entrepreneurs (and "wheeler-dealers") accounted for most of the trade in town.

Poverty was the common denominator among most of the populace. There were some "middle-class" families and several of great wealth, mostly from buying, harvesting, and shipping wood from the vast forests in the very fertile mountains and exporting them by floating rafters down the rivers to Hungary and to the Czech lands. We, the youngsters, spent several very happy occasions during summer vacations in the mountains, by actually hopping rides on those barges, made-up of huge logs tied together, with a rudder at the end, for steering. It was quite an experience. Others made substantial fortunes from exporting apples, pears, and other abundant fruits and vegetables to the industrialized lands to the west. Food was plentiful and most people did not go hungry. Meat was special, for Shabbat and *yom tov* only. Bread, beans, potatoes, onions, and other vegetables were the mainstays of the average families. Eggs, herrings, fish, and butter were in great supply. In front of at least two grocery stores stood huge barrels filled with schmaltz herrings. Everyone "fished" in them for the big fat ones. Often they formed the basis for a complete family meal in many poor people's homes.

The farmers from the outlying villages would bring in, almost daily, fresh produce, poultry, and other farm products for sale. Once a week, on Wednesdays, there was a general shopping opportunity when farmers, textile merchants, and artisans put up stalls in the main marketplace to sell or trade their wares.

Once a month there was the "big market day" or county fair, when everyone came to town, even from far-away places, to display and trade their wares. From time to time it was also the opportunity for a traveling circus and carnival to come to town and stay for several weeks. The merry-go-round and the shooting galleries were the most popular events. In addition there was also a horse market where a brisk trade in horses, for farming and hauling, took place.

I still recoil in horror when I recall one of the most frightening and dehumanizing annual events that shook me up every time I saw it happen. In the early springtime, while on my way to the

22

cheder, I was confronted by the horrible sight of the *maidel mark* (girl market). Poverty-stricken parents from the surrounding villages brought in their teenage daughters to hire them out as servants or maids to the city ladies. It was almost a slave market scene! Parents and "ladies" would argue over the merits of the girls, their fine characters and good work habits. The price was another matter for haggling. These girls were hired out for a year at a time. Often they remained in the same household for many years. It was a most degrading scene. There were tears and sobs of separation. Many would seldom, if ever, get to go back home. I recall that I was both ashamed and felt sorry for the poor girls. They were touched and examined as if they were a fattened chicken or goose. Worse, they were inspected the same as the horses on the marketplace to make sure they were strong enough to scrub the floors, do the wash and all the other household chores. Even though I knew for certain that only girls from the villages were paraded for hire (or what I always considered—for sale), I could not help worrying that my sister—and who knows, maybe someday we the boys—might also share the same fate. I suppose that in the long run these girls were actually lucky. After all, they escaped the miserable conditions of living in deprivation and starvation at home, and of sharing what little food and clothing there was at home with their many siblings. They could in fact expect to be well fed and decently clothed by their new patrons. They also had the great opportunity to live in the "metropolis," and learn the proper table manners and correct speech patterns. Still, I found it a very traumatic.

The Jewish community of Chust was established, approximately, in the late eighteenth century (in 1790 the first rabbi, Reb Yakov Grunwald, was hired). The early settlers came across the Carpathian Mountains from Western Poland or Galicia. Later on, more people came, some from the west, Hungary, Austria, Germany, and other places. They were mainly farmers, tailors, merchants, and some free professionals, such as doctors and lawyers. Some worked hard to earn a living but did not succeed. There weren't any jobs to be had in industry. The whole area was mostly populated by farmers and small cottage-industry proprietors. I recall only a few of them: There was Friedman "Der Lopatos" (wooden shovel maker); Weisz the "Etzetesh" (he made vinegar); the *"Kemal Macherin"* (made combs from animal horns); the *"Barshten Binder"* (made brushes of all kinds); the *"Beizem Macher"* (made brooms); Rosenberg *"Der Peik"* (baked bread and challahs; Kalish *"Der Zeif Mach*er" (made and sold soap). However, many others were forced to live on charity, panhandling and begging for food to support their large families.

For the most part, the Jews lived in close proximity to each other, concentrated mostly in the center of town. There were about fourteen synagogues in town. Most of them were associated with a particular sect of Hasidism. These smaller *shuls* or *shtiblech* also served as *batei midrash*—places for study groups to sit and learn day and night, as well as for *Tehilim Yidden*, plain folk who couldn't learn but were very pious and they would sit around the stove and recite Psalms most of the day. There were, however, a few very large, almost modern places of worship. I can't remember any longer all of their names or locations. All of them were truly Orthodox. There were no Conservative or Reform places of worship in town. Most men wore the traditional Hasidic garb on Shabbat, and the women wore *sheitels* or otherwise covered their hair. Even so, not everyone was observant. There just was not an organized and officially sanctioned group, community, or place of worship other than the Orthodox ones.

We also had what was commonly known as a *kehilah*, or an autonomous, Orthodox, Jewish community organization with taxation rights. All political organizations and the various Hasidic groupings were represented in the *Vaad Hakehilah*, by their legally elected deputies, in publicly held, city-wide elections. There was only one, official rabbi for the whole town. The rabbi and two *dayanim* (religious judges) made up the *beit din* (religious court) of the city. All questions of *halachah*, or disputes of any kind, were decided by one or all the members of this court. Their decisions were final, binding, and even enforceable by the civil constabulary. This system worked well not only during the democratic regime of Czechoslovakia, but also during the early years of the Hungarian occupation. The official "city rabbi" was also elected by popular vote, often only after long, heated, and partisan election campaigns that sometimes turned into very ugly arguments and even into physical violence.

The *kehilah* assessed, arbitrarily, annual taxes to be paid by all Jewish inhabitants of the community. All fees collected by the rabbi, *dayanim,* and by all other functionaries for officiating at weddings, etc., were handed over to the *kehilah* treasurer. Reluctant inhabitants who did not pay up found official city liens attached to their property or furniture. After a while, those were confiscated and eventually sold at auction to satisfy their obligation.

From these taxes and fees, the *kehilah* paid the salaries of the rabbi, the *dayanim*, and the *shochtim*, as well as the *kehilah* secretary, office staff, and maintenance. The payroll also covered the salaries of the many teachers of the city-wide Talmud Torah (supplementary Hebrew school). In addition, it maintained and paid for the three *mikvaot*, the yeshivah and cemetery upkeep, the free kitchen, as well as all other charitable, communal institutions.

The free kitchen was available for the indigent folks of the town as well as for those beggars who invaded the town every Thursday from the some 103 villages that belonged to the Chust region. The *kehilah* also provided a weekly "stipend" for those large and poor families in town who were too proud and embarrassed to go begging. During the tough days of 1940–44, the free kitchen doled out in excess of a thousand meals per day. I have first-hand knowledge of these details since my father

(ז"ל) served on the executive committee during those years (and earlier too) and he was in charge of the free kitchen and of the allotments that were doled out to the respectable needy families on the "Q.T."

I remember being given by my father a handful of sealed envelopes with addresses on them to deliver almost clandestinely (slipping them quietly under the door and running away), on Thursday evenings, that contained the monies for Shabbat meals for those families. It was with deep sorrow and anguish that I read my father's name engraved, along with the names of the other six permanent members of the executive committee of the *vaad*, in large golden letters upon a large marble slab hanging orphaned and neglected on the ransacked, desecrated, and ravaged wall of what once was the very beautiful and teeming *kehilah* office after the war. The pain was deep and lasting. That large plaque stood as a silent witness to the devastating fate that befell not just those seven pillars of the community, but the entire Jewish community and its people as well.

Besides the big, official *shul* (great synagogue), there were some other places of worship in town, some large and some very small *shtiblech*. From among the fourteen such places, I can recall only a few, primarily those that were in our immediate neighborhood or that we actually attended. By far the largest *shul* was Dos Groise Beis Medrish (the large synagogue). This full-block building had several hundred families as members and over a thousand worshipers on Shabbat and during holidays. It had a cantor, but it had no official rabbi. It was a very noisy place. Even though it was not affiliated with any particular Hasidic sect, it was nonetheless a generally Hasidic *shul* that followed the Hasidic-Sephardic form of worship rather than the Ashkenazic style of the official big *shul*.

Reb Moshe Aron's Beis Medrish was another, sizable place of worship. It had no cantor nor a rabbi. It was very old. Several of the very venerable stalwarts of town were members of that *shul*. This *shul* too, like the above mentioned one, did not identify itself with any particular Hasidic sect, but did follow the overall Hasidic-Sephardic form of worship. As was customary in town, the whole street was always referred to by the name of the *shul* that was located on it.

I know there was also a small "Cigainer *shul*" (Gypsy *shul*), named after the little street where it was located. It was very far from the center of town where we lived; therefore, I never got to see it. Next to the Cigainer *shul* was also the third *mikvah* in town. I have no idea of where it was or what it looked like.

I can't recall now the names of the rest of the synagogues or *shtiblech* in town. However, the very closest *shul* to my heart always was and always will be the beautiful Atzei Chaim Beis Medrish, where my closest friends and I grew up, played, and got into mischief together. There is no way that I can paint an accurate picture of the place, or to correctly relate the spiritual bonds that still tie me emotionally to this "*shul* of *shuls*." How we loved to watch the grown-ups "fall *korim*" (go down on their hands and knees and prostrate themselves with their faces touching the floor on Yom Kippur).

The memories become blurred and tainted by the passage of time and by the intrusion of so many other scenes of other places of worship that became part of my later experiences. However, the sights, smells, and scenes of that house of worship have helped shape my deeply rooted religious beliefs and practices, that later on served as the life-savers for me to cling to, while drowning in the stormy seas of pain and doubt, when my spiritual beliefs and basic truths faltered and I found myself sinking in the quagmire of heresy and rebellion against all the fundamental truths and practices of my youth. My soul was forever bound to that place. Like Bialik in his famous poem "*Veim Yishal Hamalach Bni Nishmatcha Ayeha?*" (And if the Angel will ask me: my son,

27

where is your soul?), I will send him to a small village, surrounded by a wall of forests with clear blue skies, and on a summer day you will see there a lonesome little boy playing by himself... young... lonely... and dreaming... that is me, my Angel... there, you will find the roots of my innocent soul... (my paraphrase). Not far from there, my dear Angel, in the Atzei Chaim Beis Medrish of *mein shtetle* Chust, my soul and spiritual self too were born, nurtured, and remained tethered to it forever.

The Atzei Chaim Beis Medrish too had no cantor or rabbi. Among its members were dozens of great talmudic scholars, some with *smicha,* and they settled on Reb Shmil Frankel, a very poor *sofer* (scribe) to serve as the unofficial rabbi. He handed down decisions on halachic matters. (This became very crucial after the great fight that surrounded the election of the last official rabbi of the town, Rabbi Yehoshua Greenwald. Rabbi Greenwald was boycotted by the members of this *shul* as well as by other sects of Hasidim. Therefore, Reb Shmil Frankel became the only *posek* [halachic authority] for the members of the shul.)

Most of the members were accomplished *baalei tefilah* (leaders of services), who took turns in leading the prayer services. My father too was a frequent choice for that honor. He was also a permanent member of the governing board and most of the time he was one of the two elected *gabaim*. For the High Holidays, too, he would sometimes lead the morning prayers (if he was not called upon to some small community out of town to lead the services there for a fee). However, for almost all of my life, until 1944, there were two main *shlichei tzibur* (service leaders for the High Holidays) in our *shul*. Reb Shmil Frankel for *Shacharit* and Reb Menashe Neuwohner and his choir, made up mostly of his seven sons, for the *Musaf* Service. Reb Menashe was one of the wealthiest people in town. He and his brother-in-law owned a very large hardware store and a cartel that controlled the hardware trade of the entire region. They also owned the Corona Hotel and lots of other properties. From those wonderfully talented seven sons, only one, my friend and *cheder*-mate Rabbi Yisroel Dovid, survived, together with his father. The oldest son, Shloime, was shot to death by the SS right before his father's eyes, witnessed by my mother and sister, during a forced retreat march from the Goerlitz concentration camp toward the final days of the war.

Reb Menashe used to pray with a grateful heart and gave thanks to G-d for all the favors that He bestowed upon him. Reb Menashe was drenched with sweat by the time he finished the services from his strenuous concentration and deep ecstasy. His seven boys adorned the seven steps leading up to the *aron hakodesh* (Holy Ark), alongside the *amud* where the *baalei tefilah* stood. Those of my close friends who survived and I constantly try to emulate, as closely as we can, whenever we are given the opportunity, the devotional and deeply emotional manner of those two dearly loved and respected *baalei tefilah*. In her later years, my beloved mother (*z"l*) used to tell me of her great yearning to hear those two people *daven* once again before she dies.

Alas, it never happened. Reb Menashe came to America and settled in Los Angeles where he did continue to *daven* on the High Holidays—but without his very special choir. The full reality of our tragic experiences during the Holocaust years hit me full force when this man, Reb Menashe, the respected and wealthy tycoon of *mein shtetle* Chust, came to visit us in Denver, on his round of cities collecting charity. He passed away in a nursing home in Yerushalayim a few years ago. During the days of his *shiva*, I had the opportunity to eulogize not just him alone, but through him also my father and the rest of their fellow Atzei Chaim stalwarts who never had a funeral or a proper burial. He became the representative, the *shaliach tzibur*, once again, for all of his contemporaries whom he had survived. Reb Shmil Frankel did not survive. To our great sorrow, this magnificent place of devotion, the Atzei Chaim Beis Medrish, was to become a place of horror and inhuman suffering later on.

The Belzer Klaus was located right across from our house in the same courtyard. It was a very small *shtibel* for the Belzer Hasidim in town. It occupied a small building of two adjacent rooms. The one in front was for the men, and the other, with a separate entrance in the back of the house, for the women. Only one of the many congregants stands out in my memory. Reb Chezkiah Greenwald was the younger brother of the great Rabbi Moshe Ben Amram Greenwald, the "*Arugas Habosem*" who served for many decades as the rabbi of our *kehilah*. I remember him well because he was a very old and frail man who used to come into our house every Yom Kippur to lie down and rest up between *Musaf* and *Mincha*. The most vivid memory I have of this greatly respected elderly man is forever engraved on my brain, as he was standing right next to me in the brickyard line-up just before being loaded into the cattle wagons and box cars for the trip to Auschwitz. Many of us had taken with us bundles of personal belongings to the unknown destination. Reb Chezkiah, perhaps eighty-five years old, took with him only a small bag containing his *talis* and *tefilin*. How will I ever forget the anguished outcry of this broken, saintly man, when one of the murderous Gestapo beasts grabbed this prized possession and drop-kicked it as if it were a football into the air with a demonic smile of pleasure registered all over his face.

"The Great Battle of the Rabbi" developed in 1933 when the rabbi of the *kehilah* at that time, the widely renown scholar Rabbi Yoseph Zvi Dushinsky (*zt"l*), decided to make *aliyah* to Eretz Yisrael, taking with him many of his disciples, to become the rabbi of the Aida Hachareidis of Yerushalayim. I was only a five-year-old boy at the time, but I remember vividly how he gave each and every child his personal blessings before departing town. (He was also the *sandek* at my *bris*.)

A search for a suitable candidate and an intensive election campaign began to find a proper replacement for the Rav. As usual, many different parties and Hasidic groupings came up with their own worthy candidates.

The campaign heated up and became terribly ugly. People chose sides, argued, and became enemies. Windows of opponents were smashed and fistfights broke out among the partisans of the two candidates. The fact that the two candidates were related made no difference. Name-calling became routine on both sides. Terrible, libelous rumors and wild stories were spread around about the character, or lack of it, concerning the younger candidate.

We were intimately involved in the heat of the election campaign. We watched our father putting his very considerable talents as an amateur writer and poet in Yiddish and in Hebrew at the service of the Popper Rav, as he was commanded by his Rebbe to do. He wrote and published beautiful pamphlets and handbills in prose and in poetic form, exalting the virtues of the candidate and denigrating those of his contemporary, and former classmate and friend, Reb "Shea." It gave father pangs of a guilty conscience to have turned against his erstwhile friend, but you just did not dare to disobey the Rebbe's wishes and directives. Later on, when the chips were down, both my father and the rest of our family were destined to pay a very heavy price for this blind obedience and total subjugation to the Rebbe's dictates, and for his absolute conviction of his infallibility.

The day of the public elections of a rabbi arrived. The secret ballots were cast at city hall under the watchful eyes of the city constabulary, guarding against fraudulent ballot stuffing. Rabbi Yehoshua Greenwald was installed as the official rabbi of Chust, by order of the governor. He arrived in Chust all the way from Ungvar with a full escort of state policemen protecting him. Pictures of that scene added fuel to the fire of the battle and served as additional evidence that he was unworthy to sit on the lofty "throne" of his illustrious forefathers and predecessors.

The Satmarer Rebbe ordered his followers to completely ignore the new rabbi and have no confidence in his halachic decrees and decisions. He declared him to be *tameh* (ritually unclean). He forbade his followers to eat any meat that was sold under the rabbi's supervision. He stopped just short of putting the rabbi in *cherem* (excommunication). When his opponents, under the fiat of the Satmarer Rebbe, resorted to importing kosher meat and poultry from out of town, the *kehilah* obtained an official city ordinance forbidding such practices (on account that it deprived the *kehilah* treasury of fees and taxes).

Ironically, both the Satmarer Rebbe and the Chuster Rav survived the Holocaust in different ways and both settled in Brooklyn. Reb Yehoshua Greenwald established the Chuster *shul* in Boro Park and published many important halachic responsa books. Many of his halachic decisions deal with questions that arose during the years of persecution and in the concentration camps (such as "is one allowed to escape and save himself knowing full well that the Nazis will retaliate by executing many hostages?") He called his *sefarim* "Chesed Yehoshua." Of tremendous interest to me and to many others is the foreword to his first *sefer*, called "*Ayin Dimah*" (The wellspring of tears). In it he describes, poignantly and in heart-rending detail, the innermost thoughts and emotions of a community Rav seeing and helplessly agonizing over the destruction of his beloved community, and the time that he spent in various concentration camps. It is a very powerful testimony. It was translated into English and published in an American Jewish periodical. How tragic the irony, and for me the agony as well, of seeing how the Satmarer Rebbe befriended and drew close to him the very same "*tameh*" Reb Yehoshua, whom my father was compelled to berate and degrade on the Rebbe's command. He had him sit by his right side at public functions, as if nothing ever happened. What was that sanctimonious tumult all about? How did this very same despised person become an honored friend? The "Idol" (the Rebbe), it seems, had clay feet, after all. It was all a farce and a cruel political game. Too bad many fine people got hurt in the dirty process.

Jewish education was considered paramount and universal. I can't imagine that there might have been any Jewish boy in town who did not receive a Jewish education of one intensity or another. For the poorer boys there was the *kehilah*-sponsored, tuition-free Talmud Torah school, with its over-crowded classes and impatient teachers and poorly behaved students. However, the more affluent people sent their boys to private *cheder*-type schools. These were one-room, storefront, kind of makeshift classrooms. The parents had to pay monthly tuition directly to the teachers. For the most part they had a limited number of spaces available which meant smaller classes with more individual attention to every boy. This style of school was popular because here you had a selection of a number of different teachers to choose from. And since parents had to pay tuition, the teachers made sure to be accountable to the parents.

I have never been inside the Talmud Torah building, and I can't describe what went on there. All of my elementary school years were spent in the *cheder*-type schools, in addition to attendance in the "regular," government-established, public school.

Boys began to go to *cheder* or to the Talmud Torah at age four. Attendance in class lasted from very early in the morning until late in the evening, with time out to go to the regular, non-Jewish public schools. The differences between the two types of school were phenomenal. At the public schools, the teachers smiled and instructed instead of yelling and hitting. It was warm, friendly, and light. There was order and whispering. There was music, art, gym, field trips, pictures and posters on the walls. Here, every student had a desk instead of the long table and rickety benches of the *cheder*. Here, we didn't take turns bringing firewood to class for the iron stove in the winter and kerosene for the lamps. (These stark differences between the two kinds of schools were a constant irritation to me. I wouldn't be surprised to find out that I developed a great need within my psyche to become a "regular" Hebrew teacher in a "regular" setting). Here, we actually saw girls our own age and did not have to turn the other way. Since there were compulsory attendance laws to comply with, there was, alas, no choice but to mingle and even speak on occasion with a girl. This of course was not possible in the Jewish school because Jewish education was for the males of the species only!

In the late 1930s, a sort of a belated "Renaissance" arrived to town. A Hebrew, Zionist, elementary day school was established. Almost none of the Hasidim would allow their children to attend that co-educational place of study. Very few were brave enough to go against the mainstream consensus and send their children to that Hebrew school. I can't remember, but I think that the school grew and expanded into a high school. I was not allowed to attend that Zionist school since I was destined to become a *yeshivah bochur* and, eventually, a real talmudic scholar.

My memory fails me to pinpoint the exact year, but a girls-only, Beth Jacob–type school was also established in town. Even though this was an ultra-religious school, it was boycotted by most of the stalwarts and the guardians of the *hasidic* tradition based on the argument that Torah study is too dangerous for women! In fact, among the posted by-laws of our *shul*, there was a clear admonition that anyone who sends their daughter to the Beth Jacob school will forfeit the right to be a member. So were those who would allow members of the family to go to the movies or to a theater performance. (Periodically, itinerant Yiddish repertoire performing troops visited our town.)

There were a great number of Torah scholars in Chust. Quite a few had *smicha* to be rabbis but chose not to make Torah a trade tool. There were very few complete ignoramuses, since every man, without exception, knew how to read the prayers and even to review the weekly Torah reading portion from the original

34

Hebrew texts. The women, however, had to rely often on the one lady who knew how to read the prayers aloud in the women's section and the others followed along.

There were some people who believed in ridiculous superstitions that belonged to the dark ages, in addition to the usual, run-of-the-mill kinds that are common to most people of very deep and blind faith. Most folks had a complete and abiding belief that there are ghosts and demons all around us, waiting for us to err in our ways, and they would immediately pounce upon us and hurt us badly or would enter our bodies and take possession of our souls too. The *dibbuk* was a very familiar "being" in our town as well as in most, if not in all *shtetlech* and villages of our regions. This belief became reinforced by the presence in our city of quite a few totally deranged, perhaps "possessed" men and women. A few are hard to forget. We, the children, were very cruel to them. We ran after them in the streets, calling them crazy and degrading names.

"*Leibelle-Shir-a-Baba*" was the name and label attached to one of those unfortunate human beings. He was a slightly built person. Dressed in rags and constantly conversing with himself aloud, he roamed the streets all day long foraging for food. The children would taunt and tease him mercilessly.

"Sender-with-the-Bender" was a huge man dressed in shredded rags. Hence the epithet of "Bender"—ribbons. He was a real menace. When running after him in the streets in packs and taunting him, we kept a respectable distance to afford us a head start lest he suddenly turn and run after us. Pity to the poor kid who was slow in retreat. No one looked after him either. Did he have family or relatives? These human beings were abandoned by G-d and by their fellow Jews and by the community at large. They were simply left on their own.

"*Kutchke-Toba*" was the female version of the former two. She too roamed the streets talking and arguing with herself, or perhaps with all of us and probably with her Creator too. She was almost middle-aged, dressed in torn and profusely patched up nondescript garments. Her being a woman did not bestow upon her special protection from us. We ran after her and taunted her as equal-opportunity offenders!

There were many others whom I have already forgotten. There was another one who was a real menace to everyone. I think he was the one called "*Chayim-Coocoo-Madar.*" People said that he was a former army officer who became raving mad. He ran around town yelling and threatening people, young and old, with an unsheathed sword in hand. No one dared come near him. There was also the very meek and sedate "Yankele" who always stood at the same spot in front of his parents' inn. I remember him being a man in his mid-thirties. He was somewhat of an idiot-savant. He could recite accurately complete passages not only from the Bible, but also from the Talmud. Rumor had it that he became mad "from knowing too much."

Some of the abnormal superstitions were real gems. Since the big *shul*, across from us in the *kehilah-hoif,* had no *mezuzot* affixed to its doorposts, to protect it from being taken over at night by various *sheidim* (demons and ghosts), we were certain that the nights belonged to them. We were sure that the ghosts gather in the *shul* at midnight to hold services. We were also warned by our friends that if we hear our names called up to the Torah in our sleep, we must rise, put on our garments backward, walk backward into the *shul*, walk up backward to the Torah reading table, and recite the blessings backward. Only then could we escape the horrible suffering that they would otherwise inflict upon us. Many nights I was reluctant to go to bed and fall asleep, fearing the terror that might overtake me if and when it would come my turn to be so "honored" by my ghostly neighbors from across the street. My only hope was that they would realize that I am not yet a Bar Mitzvah boy and therefore ineligible to be called up to the Torah. Luckily, as I matured a little more and came closer to that age I also became less afraid (I found in the Talmud many special sayings that would keep them away from me), and I realized that not all stories and superstitions are based on facts.

There was no hospital or clinic in town. For serious illnesses one had to travel to a hospital in Beregszasz, which was far away. However, there were quite a few very capable physicians in town. Most of them were Jewish. One of the non-Jewish doctors, Dr. Erpf, joined the German SS (he was an ethnic German). He was caught and executed after the war for his war crimes. He, of course, was the exception. The others were kind and caring professionals. Dr. Wasserman was a very kindly, grandfather type pediatrician slightly bent over with old age, sporting a prominent mustache, who not only made house calls to the sick children, but made sure that the family had the money to purchase the medications and food for everyone. He too perished in Auschwitz.

There were no newspapers published in town. The ones available in the tobacco kiosks came from far away and were usually a day or two late. Some people subscribed to papers and magazines by mail. Very few people had radios in their homes. The ones that I recall seeing and hearing were big table-top or floor-standing models with two big knobs for tuning and volume control. I have no idea where the broadcasts originated from. I do remember that they whistled and crackled with static and it was not always clear enough to understand. We, the kids, were convinced beyond any doubt that there were tiny people inside those boxes whose voices we heard. We speculated as to who they were and when they come out of those boxes to eat. When the war broke out, neighbors from near and far would gather to the lucky owners of one of those radios to listen, question the narrators on missed words or incomplete sentences, as if they could be heard by the narrator, and then spend a great deal of time speculating, arguing, and interpreting what they each thought they heard and understood.

Telephones were the prized possessions of a very select few large stores and even fewer individuals. The rest of us, if and when the urgent need arose to speak to someone out of town (in town you had no need to phone; you just walked over and delivered the message in person), you went to the main post office and filled out a summons-like form stating whom you want to get in touch with, in what city, and the exact day and time. The post office in the target city would summon that individual to appear at the post office in their own town, at the appointed day and time, and both parties would wait there for a successful connection. I must have been at least about eight to ten years old when my father took me along to the post office to witness and even participate in such an event. I was the envy of all of my friends. I actually got to shout "Hello" over the phone to a Mr. Ament, in Kosice, a large city in Slovakia, about 150 kilometers away!

Most homes had iceboxes with large chunks of ice hauled by hand from the ice factory in them, to keep food from spoiling. We didn't have one. We had two ways to preserve food. If it was just for the next day, it was placed on the cold cement floor of the spacious pantry (the *shpeiss*). The large, walk-in pantry was a storehouse for food supplies both raw and cooked.

Food that needed immediate refrigeration (like cooked fish, and soup for Shabbat, were put, while still hot, on the damp dirt floor of the common cellar that was also used by all of the other dwellers in our court. The cellar was underneath the "Belzer Klaus," a *shtibel* where the Belz Hasidim prayed. The *shtibel* was on top of a wooden stairway with a wooden banister. We used to play on the stairs' landing and inside the *shtibel*. One day, as we were playing on top of the stairs, one of our little friends, Benzi Zoldan, slid down the banister, unaware of the terrible fate that awaited him downstairs. There was a huge, rusty nail protruding at the very bottom of the rail. His screaming and profuse bleeding shattered the entire neighborhood, not just our court dwellers.

Needless to say, he became somewhat of a celebrity in town. None of us ever again slid down on that banister or on any other. He never came back from Auschwitz.

That cellar kept food well and fresh and safe, as long as people remembered to put heavy rocks or bricks on the lids of the pots to keep the rats from feasting on the food. Watermelons and other such large fruits were kept cool by lowering them with the long, counter-weighted swing-arm above the well in a bucket, parking them at the bottom of the well for several hours, and then "fishing" them up by the hook at the tip of that long arm.

This was *mein shtetle* Chust. It is forever gone. These days, I often entertain myself with thoughts about what life would have been like for us if we would not have been uprooted from home and family. What would I have turned out to be? Would I have continued to live in the "dark ages" of Chust? Would I have continued in my father's footsteps? Would I have continued to worship the Satmarer Rebbe? Would I have been wearing a caftan and *shtreimel*, as all of my predecessors did for countless generations? Would "enlightenment" have ever struck us too? What kinds of turns would my future have taken? I will never know. Maybe it is best that I don't know.

MY FAMILY

My immediate family consisted of:

- My father, David Rosenfeld (killed in the Buchenwald concentration camp)
- My mother, Chanah (Chantshi), *née* Lebowitz (survived Auschwitz)
- My sister, Leah (Leitchu) (survived Auschwitz)
- My brother, Yoel (Yolika) (perished at age 13 in Auschwitz)
- Myself, Israel (Sruli) (survived Auschwitz)

My father's grandfather, Reb Naftali Rosenfeld, came to Teich as a young man from Raisha (Brzezhov) in Poland, escaping forced military service in that country. This was around the middle of the nineteenth century.

Reb Naftali had four sons and two daughters:

My grandfather, Reb Aryeh Leibish Rosenfeld, married Mindya Rivka Fishman, the sister of Reb Elimelech Fishman, the Gabbai of Reb Shayele Kerestirer, one the most famous Hasidic masters of Hungary. He also wrote a *sefer* called *Lechem Abirim*. They had two sons and three daughters.

The second son of Reb Naftali Rosenfeld was my uncle Moshe Rosenfeld. He settled in Chust. He was famous for his wisdom and for his great influence on the civil authorities in intervening on their behalf. He was known as "Moshe Teicher."

Reb Naftali's third son was Favish. He lived next door to my grandfather in Teich. I do not know if any of his descendants remained alive after the Holocaust.

40

Reb Naftali's fourth son was Shmuel Chaim. He lived in Vilchowitz and had a large family. Many of them survived and settled in Israel.

I have no first-hand knowledge of the history of the two daughters.

My grandparents had three sons and three or four daughters:

- The oldest son was Moshe. He lived in Chust. Some of his children survived.
- The second son was Zeida. He lived in Teich. Some of his children survived.
- The youngest son was my father, Reb Dovid Rosenfeld. He was a very talented, handsome, and congenial man. He grew up in Teich and had many close friends there.

At a young age, as was the custom of the day, my father left Teich to study in the yeshivah in Orshava that was headed by Reb Yolish Teitelbaum. He moved with him to Krule in Rumania. Reb Yolish later on became the famous Satmarer Rebbe. My father spent over ten years learning with Reb Yolish.

Of all of my father's sisters, we were very close only with one of them, Mime (aunt) Sheindel Kahan and her husband. They had two very handsome and talented sons, Tuly (Naftali) and Yumi (Binyamin), and one daughter, Etu. We loved them dearly. It was always a joy to visit with them and when they came to visit with us. None of the entire family survived the Holocaust.

Another sister, Chaya Sarah (Hella Neni), married a Mr. Horowitz and lived in Munkatch. I don't recall visiting them more than once or twice, but she often came to visit with us. No one survived the war of that family either.

The third sister, Mime Feiga, married and lived in a small village in Rumania called Nyigresht. We never visited them, nor did they ever come to visit us. However, I do remember father visiting them several times.

The fourth sister, Etya, never married, or perhaps was widowed, but since I can recall, she lived with my grandparents in Teich.

We always loved to visit our grandparents in Teich. We would dress up in our finest clothes and pack a feast for the one-hour-long train ride. As soon as the train pulled out of the station, we became hungry and began the ceremony of unpacking the food bundle and eating the fried chicken and all the other goodies that we brought along for the trip.

As mentioned above, Reb Moshe Teicher was the son of Reb Naftali. He married a woman from Chust and settled there. He was a very unique and imposing personality. He looked very much like his brother, Leibish, big and impressive. He was a wealthy man but lived on a very modest standard. He had a tiny grocery store in front of his very small house in the *Meiches gass*, which was mostly run by his wife, and a huge wholesale grocery warehouse run by his son-in-law Reb Shea Fish. Reb Moshe became known far and wide by his nickname "Reb Moshe Teicher" (from Teich). He never spent any time attending to his business affairs. He was the classic *klal-tuer* (working for the benefit of his fellow men, altruistically), the true *shtadlan* (advocate) for the needy and all who got themselves in a bind with the authorities. Jew and non-Jew alike would come knocking on his door, at all hours of the day or night, crying their hearts out and begging him to intervene on their behalf before the various government departments. One had a tax problem, the other had a license problem, the third one had a son who was drafted to the army but was needed desperately to plow the fields, etc. Everyone left his presence with the full confidence that Reb Moshe would take care of everything. And he did. He never bribed any officials, yet they were like putty in his hands. It was phenomenal. Here was the very personification of the Jewish caricature: he wore a long *kapota*, a full, lengthy, unkempt beard, long *tzitzis* (fringes) hanging out, big heavy boots

42

on his feet, summer and winter, a round flat felt hat on his head. Yet any official—from the deputy governor, who presided over the vast bureaucracy of the Chust region, to the city mayor, to the military commandant of the district, to the judges and constables on the beat—melted away before his tremendous charm and wisdom. I have heard many times that when he would appear at a high office to intercede on behalf of one of his petitioners, the mayor or the official in charge would actually get up from behind his desk and allow him to do as he pleased. All the books were opened to him.

My mother's family lived in Sekernitze, a small village about eight to ten kilometers outside of Chust, just off the railroad tracks that lead from Chust to Teich. In fact it was the very first train stop on that track. Only several hundred people lived there, among them perhaps as many as 200 Jews. My mother's father, Reb Ezra (Halevi) Lebowits, married Sure Reise Lax from Sighet and they settled in Chust. The rest of that family stayed on in Sekernitze. My grandfather's brother, Reb Pinchas Lebowits, was a wealthy landowner and the proprietor of the large mill, traffic (tobacco store), liqueur wholesaler, and grocery store. He lived just across the railroad station and we could see his big house from the train on our journeys to Teich. He was a life-saver to us during the very hard times of 1942–44, when bread and other staples such as oil, flour, and corn meal were strictly rationed and sometimes completely unavailable at any price; he would always find a way, at the risk of jail, to keep us supplied with those staples generously. Some of his sons and grandchildren survived and live in New York.

I don't know how many siblings there were in my grandfather's family. I remember that one of his sisters married a Mr. Adler and lived in Sekernitze. One of their sons, Moty Adler, lived in New York and had a button factory. One of their daughters, Machle Shtauber, lives in Bnei Brak.

I don't know what my grandfather did for a living, probably the same thing as most others in town—nothing in particular. He likely earned some money from being a middleman, buying and selling whatever some people wanted to sell and others wanted to buy, earning a slight mark-up fee. My grandparents had five sons and two daughters:

1) Leibish (Yehudah?). He left for America with his father as a scholarly young man. I got to know him only when I came to America in 1948. My grandfather stayed in the United States. From time to time he would send home a few dollars, but he never returned home. Several times he sent affidavits and steamship tickets for the family to come to America, but my grandmother never took advantage of the offer to emigrate. My grandfather and Leibish must have left for America around 1910 or so, since my mother, who was the youngest, was born in 1902, and she was a very small child at the time and couldn't remember her father at all.

Grandmother was a very dour and "regal" ramrod-straight lady. I can't recall her ever laughing aloud. She was always serious. She managed to send her five sons to the best *yeshivot*. All of her five sons received *heter horaah* (rabbinic ordination). She would tell me with tremendous pride about the real scholarship and the great *nachas* (joy) that she derived from each of her children.

I recall her very modest home consisting of one room that was a combination kitchen, dining room, living room, and bedroom. Another very small room had two beds in it. This room she would rent out, from time to time, to yeshivah students and others who needed room and board. There was no electricity in her home and, of course, no running water either. Whenever mother or any of her better-off brothers would come to visit grandmother, they would always find the right opportunity when she wasn't looking and they put some large money bills under one special cup on the top of the cupboard so as not to embarrass her. It was amazing to behold the tremendous respect and love that her children had for her.

Grandfather collapsed and died on a Brooklyn street sometime before the outbreak of the Second World War. He is buried somewhere in the Long Island Jewish Cemetery. Feter Leibish became an "operator"—ladies' garment sewing machine operator. He remained a poor man and lived in Long Island City, Queens, "projects." When mother made contact with him after the war (traced by the Joint Distribution Committee), he shared with us what little he had. It was of tremendous assistance to us. He also sent an "affidavit" for mother to be able to come to the States. He passed away sometime in the 1950's.

2) Their second son was Reb Yisroel Dovid. He became a *shochet* in Kalin, a small village somewhere in Carpathia. He had a houseful of children and very little income. None of that entire family (about eight to nine children) survived the Holocaust.

3) Their third son, Feter Yekel (Yaakov) was the *dayan* of Kapush, a small town near Ungvar. He was a great scholar and a famous *posek*. He learned for about twenty years with the very famous Kashoer Rav, Reb Shaul Brach. He received *heter horaah* from Reb Shaul Brach and also from Rav Dushinsky (the only person ever to receive such a great honor, only on the behest of his mentor, Reb Shaul Brach). We were always so proud when he visited us. We used to go around and show off to our friends the special silver-handled walking cane that was the status symbol of the rabbi or the *dayan*. He too had a house full of children. In Budapest, after the war was over, he headed an especially constituted *"Bet-Din Le Tikun Agunoth"* (a Jewish court to free the women who survived from remaining in "limbo," not having proof of their husbands' deaths, unable to remarry). When he arrived in America, he became the *dayan* of the Satmar community in Williamsburg, Brooklyn, and head of the Central Rabbinical Congress's Kashruth and Halachah Department. He wrote many tomes on *halachah*. Four volumes were published recently, by the name of *Mishnas Yaakov*.

4) Feter Yoel was the liveliest and funniest of all five brothers. He was always in a jovial mood, no matter how bad the situation. He too was an accomplished talmudic scholar, but he chose to earn a living by selling yard goods, for ladies garments. He was not a wealthy man but he lived comfortably. He used to put up stalls to sell his textiles during the weekly market days and would take his stall and merchandise, loaded on a hired horse-drawn wagon, to other towns when they had their big market days. It was not an easy way to earn a living, but this was the common practice of all small merchants of the region. We all loved Feter Yoel dearly. He was great fun to be with and would entertain us with jokes and little magic tricks. He came to our house very often. He was with me during part of the time in Auschwitz. He didn't survive.

One of his sons, Hersh Leib, survived and very mysteriously disappeared a few days after the liberation by the British Army. No one knew what happened to him for about fifteen years. Then, suddenly, my Feter Yekel of Brooklyn received a letter from him from Karaganda, Kazakhstan (or Uzbekistan?), in Russian Central Asia! Unceremoniously the Russians had taken him to a holding camp for deserters and shipped him off to the coal mines of Asia. He was all of seventeen years old at the time! He worked the coal mines for several years till he developed a lung problem. When he kept protesting to the authorities that he was a prisoner in a German concentration camp, he was told that if he could work for the Germans, he could also work for them. When he became ill, they released him from the mining camp and he learned how to be a locksmith. He met a Jewish girl from Pinsk (or Minsk?); they got married and settled in Karaganda. He had no idea if any one of his parents or many siblings survived.

His wife encouraged him to apply for permission to travel to Chust, which was by now an integral part of Soviet Ukraine. He finally received permission and unsuccessfully attempted to reclaim his parents' property. But while in Chust he met Moshe Lebowits in Sekernice, the son of Feter Pinchas. Moshe knew all about who survived from the family and gave him Feter Yekel's address. That's when he found out that his parents didn't survive but that two of his sisters did. They both had settled in Israel. All of us in the U.S. were sending him packages of clothing and other durable goods to Russia. He finally came for a two-month visit to Israel. He was convinced that the abundance of food and clothes displayed in the stores were not for sale but only for propaganda purposes. His absolute proof was the fact that no one stood in line at those stores to actually purchase anything! The power of brainwashing can't be underestimated. He was also convinced that my mother's apartment was "bugged" and that the K.G.B. was following him and listening in on his conversations. He would tell of his terrible ordeals only to trusted family members and only in the open streets. He refused to come to settle in Israel because he would lose his pension rights from Russia.

Some years later, when things became unstable in Russia and his son Moshe, a physician, and his daughter and her parents decided to emigrate to Israel, he and his wife too finally came. They settled in Karmiel, in the Galilee.

5) Feter Hershel Lebowits was the fifth son of Reb Ezra and Sure Reise. He was a very learned man. He too had *heter horaah* but chose to become, like his older brother, a yard goods merchant. He married the daughter of a well-to-do merchant, Mr. Katz of Teich, and they settled there. Feter Hershel had a very sharp and analytical mind. He was well off financially too. He did not travel the market-stall circuit as did his older brother. As a matter of fact, when it became clear that we would all be deported and all valuables would be confiscated, he came to Chust and gave every one of his siblings gold coins, diamonds, and other valuables to take with them. He also buried a large cache of gold coins somewhere in the backyard of his home in Teich. Alas, someone

found this treasure and took it before their only son, Yide Yoel (Prof. Joel Lebowits), could get to it after the war. Their only daughter, Freidi, did not survive. Neither did their parents.

Joel survived the war even though he was two years younger than me. He was only fourteen years old at the time of liberation. After spending some time learning at the Vizhnitzer Yeshivah in Grosswerdan, Rumania, he came to a D.P. camp in Germany. From there he was brought to America as a student of Mesivta Torah Vodaas in Brooklyn. He was always known to have an exceptionally sharp mind. He was an *iluy* (genius). Even when we studied together in the same yeshivah before the war, he was always at least two years ahead of me in his progress, even though he was two years my junior. He finished high school at Torah Vodaas in Brooklyn. In spite of the pleas and promises of the yeshivah deans to continue his Torah studies there, he firmly decided to go on to college. He graduated from Brooklyn College after just two years, *summa cum laude* and a member of the Phi Beta Kappa honor society. He also worked as a waiter during those two years to support himself. This was quite a feat! In his early twenties he received his Ph.D. in theoretical physics and advanced mathematics. For about twenty-five years or so he was head of the Graduate School of Science at Yeshiva University and the editor of the *Scripta Mathematica* publication. During all of those years he was under permanent contract to do advanced research for the U.S. Air Force. He represented them at international conferences. He has flown around the world in Air Force planes. He spent time as guest lecturer at the Sorbonne, the universities of Moscow and Leningrad, Peking, Tapei, Tel Aviv, Haifa, the Weitzman Institute, etc. He now holds a full professorship at Rutgers University of New Jersey. He has remained his very kind, sweet, and shy Yide Yoel that we loved so much as a child.

6) Mime Maryim was the older of the two daughters of my grandparents, Reb Ezra and Sure Reise. She married Reb Mordechai

Zelkovits. They lived in Chust not far from grandmother's home. Feter Mordechai also had a yard goods store. He too traveled the market circuit. It was a tough way to earn a living. I recall as a child bringing pots with hot burning coals to the stalls on market days for both of my uncles, Yoel and Mordechai, to warm their hands over them during the harsh winter days. Mordechai too was a learned man. They had a full house of children. From the entire family only Yehuda (Leibi) and Moshe survived. They both live in Jerusalem. Moshe became in charge over all of the Jewish holy places in Israel.

7) My mother, Chana (Chantshi, or Haynalka), was the youngest of the seven siblings. She didn't have a happy childhood. She learned wig making from her older sister. She was somewhat of a rebel and a free spirit. She was extremely bright, intelligent, and had an insatiable thirst to know "things." She was a straight-A student during all her school years. Even though it was unheard of among her peers and in her circles, she insisted on graduating from a Hungarian public high school. For a girl from an ultra-Orthodox home this was considered an unforgivable breach of the convention. She was very proud of this achievement. She read books and news magazines. She went to the movies and to theater performances. She certainly had a mind of her own and did whatever she deemed to be right, even in the face of criticism from others.

From age fourteen or so, she became the main breadwinner for her family. She made sure that there was enough food for the family even when she had to smuggle flour in her bloomers across the borders from Rumania during World War I, when she was a mere teenager. The police would constantly harass her and grandmother to find out where the five brothers were hiding from military service. She worked all day and even into the nights, during her free time from school, making and combing wigs for the ultra-Orthodox women in town. In time she became the most sought after wig-maker not just in town but also in the surrounding villages and townships. Like with everything else she did in life she perfected her craft too. She never knew that one could get by with less than total dedication and perfection.

The fact that she never knew her father gave her a lot of sorrow. I think she never found out why he left for America or why grandmother never followed him with the rest of the family. I think the subject was taboo and never discussed. It must have been a great burden for mother to carry as she grew up. It did give her, however, the impetus to stand on her own feet and work hard to achieve her self-imposed goals. She had many close girlfriends with whom she kept up with friendship even in later years.

Mother was a strikingly beautiful young lady. She had many suitors. She dressed smartly and was also a very pleasant and interesting conversationalist on almost any topic of currency or literature as well as history and other cultural topics.

Father met mother while he was studying in Chust at the yeshivah. They actually met and spoke to each other. This was unheard of in those days and in those circles. I don't know how it came about, with or without the traditional services of a *shadchan*; they became engaged and got married in 1924, mother being twenty-two and father four years older. They settled in Chust. Mother continued working, making (actually manufacturing from scratch) wigs. Father opened a little "bodega" store. It never produced enough income to provide for the needs of the family. In time he sold the almost bankrupt store and began searching for ways to earn some money. He was never very successful. He tried wholesale apple buying and selling ("futures"). Then he speculated with cabbage buying and selling. He did the same with gold and foreign currency (which was not very legal). He tried selling *lulovim* and *etrogim* (he lost a bundle when a crate full of *etrogim* from Greece arrived late). He tried wholesale chocolate and candy selling.

Later on when everything else failed (not because of ineptness or lack of intelligence, but due to the terrible economic situation of the late 1920's and early 1930's), he became an insurance agent for Etna Life Insurance Co.

When the Battle of the Rabbi began, father and some others of his friends learned to become *shochtim*. All of this time mother continued to make wigs. Some nights, prior to holidays, mother would actually work through the night, without any sleep! Father suffered silently but was helpless. He could never replace the income mother brought in. He ate himself on the inside. He was terribly embarrassed having to live off mother's earnings. Mother continued working until the onslaught of the Holocaust and even after it.

In 1927 my sister Lea (Leitchu) was born. In 1928 I came along. Our little brother, Yoel (Yolika), was born two years later. We lived in several different houses in the same courtyard, during different stages of our lives. They were rented houses. Each one was an improvement and an upgrade over the previous one.

In addition, each tenant was assigned one latrine, one woodshed (where we stored the firewood all year long, plus several cages with chickens, that were force-fed to fatten them up for the schmaltz, especially for Pesach), plus a fairly large section of the huge garden in the back of the house, where everyone planted vegetables for their tables.

Since we had no central heating, only the wood burning stoves, when we went to bed on cold winter nights, our parents put a hot brick wrapped in a towel, or a rubber bottle with hot water, at our feet to keep us warm.

EARLY CHILDHOOD

In spite of the fact that mother was the main provider for the family, making and styling ladies wigs, we had a fairly tranquil and nurturing home. The three of us never felt deprived of anything that we needed. Food was always plentiful. Mother was a terrific cook and she always found time to prepare meals. Shabbat was always a festive and truly joyful day in our home. I recall with nostalgia the warmth of the atmosphere. Mother finally had the time to relax and sit at the festive table without rushing. In the winter, Friday nights were especially memorable. We dined by the Shabbat candle lights gently flickering. Everyone participated in singing *zemirot*. The "Shabbat Goy" would come and stoke the fire in the iron stove. Even when the candles burned out, the light from the red-hot stove shed a gentle, mysterious glow over the dining room with shadows dancing on the walls. We all gathered around the stove, put our heads on father's and mother's laps and sang sweet and melancholy ballads in Yiddish and in Hebrew. Some were original compositions or translations created by father. Others were old, standard Yiddish folk songs and tear-jerkers. Father would become so sentimental that his tears would flow and he would hug us tightly and pat our heads lovingly. He was a romantic and had a very caring heart. He was not embarrassed to cry and show his feelings. He was very hurt by the fact that he could not provide financially for the family. I remember him asking mother many times to stop working and that he would find a way to support us. However, it never happened, and it bothered him deeply. He was a habitual fingernail biter.

Our home was almost always filled with women who brought their wigs to be fixed, and others who just came to talk with mother. The kitchen was always teeming with people. The prevalent languages spoken were Hungarian and Yiddish. Mother always spoke Hungarian with her customers and with my sister Leitchu. Father always spoke to us in Yiddish only, even though he spoke Hungarian fluently. In the winter, especially on Saturday nights, the house was filled with friends and neighbors. We played many different kinds of table games, cards, chess, etc. Father always managed to bring in joy and happiness during those family times together.

I was very happy and proud to go *shpatziren* (strolling) with my father in the streets and in the marketplaces. Young adults, as well as others in town, would seek out his company for advice and for his opinions on the events of the world and to enjoy his jokes and stories. He was truly "the life of the party" with his witticisms, songs, and parodies. He always walked with a cane (hooked up on one shoulder and held with one hand from the back. It was purely a prop, and trademark of the "man of the world." It was not utilitarian at all.). In the winter he wore a heavy coat adorned with an expensive nutria fur collar, and a Persian lamb's fur hat. With his regal looking full beard and deep-set eyes he was a very noticeable person.

This bonding between my father and me became strongest when in 1943 I could no longer travel out of town to study. Whenever he could, he would teach me some special interpretations of complex passages of the Torah, Rashi, and Talmud. He taught me how to look beyond the surface and search for deeper and more profound meanings and answers. Oh, how I cherished those precious opportunities, holding hands as we walked and talked. He taught me how to write and how to read "between the lines." He would also share with me the family history. This special relationship intensified many fold while we were together in the Auschwitz and later on in the Buna camps. He also had a great love for Leitchu, because she was very bright, pretty, popular, and a quick study. She always wanted to learn Talmud, and would sit and absorb everything that father and I were learning or discussing, asking good questions, and providing insights into complex problems.

Alas, Yolika was not the student of the family. He was very bright, but didn't try to compete with Leitchu and me in learning. He was content to be cute and cuddly. He was a consummate businessman. He "borrowed" money from mother's work table and lent it to his friends with interest, ever since he was a very young child.

Grandmother always spent most of the summer in a rented cabin in the mountains. Soymie, next to Volovo, was one of the favorite spas for the Jewish people of Chust. It was set in a beautiful valley, between two mountain ranges that were only a few hundred yards apart from each other. A swift, fairly deep and wide river of clear and cool water flowed along the valley. It had healing springs of bubbling, sparkling, and naturally carbonated, mineral waters. The waters were delicious and smelled of phosphorus and other minerals. It was also heated and used for curing mineral baths to take care of all kinds of ailments. The water was heated in huge boilers with lots of fragrant boughs of fir trees in it. The campsite was almost like a frontier outpost. Several long log-barracks were divided into many one-room cabins, one per family. You could actually hear and sometimes even see from one cabin to the next. The bathhouse was also a long log cabin divided into smaller cabins with five to six wooden tubs in each of them. The hot water came by way of a long wooden "shoot" with plugged up holes in front of each tub. When you needed more hot water, you would yell aloud to the attendant to send more hot water. You would then block off the shoot with a paddle-like stopper and pull out the plug in front of your tub.

It was a very beautiful and relaxing place. In the mornings we watched the deer and the antelopes come down from the mountains to quench their thirst at the river. During the day we would climb the mountains and pick all sorts of berries and hazelnuts. For most of the summer Leitchu would share the cabin and the tub with grandmother. However, from time to time all three of us and our parents too would come out for a vacation. It was absolutely soothing and restoring both to the flesh and to the spirit. Sometimes we would rent a regular room in a house in the village for more space and better privacy.

I was the worst possible problem when it came to food. I was a finicky and fussy eater. There were foods that I just refused to even taste. The first thing I did when coming home from school was to peek into the pots on the stove to investigate what was cooking. Sometimes I even skipped that process, by just proclaiming loudly as I entered into the kitchen: "What's that horrible stench?" Very often, I would sit by myself, away from the table, and just eat bread with a layer of sugar or jam in place of the meals that mother prepared. No meat, except chicken, was ever permitted in the house. Geese, turkeys, and ducks were also forbidden (by me).

As siblings, we got along as well as any siblings might. We fought, we argued, and we loved each other very much. Mother put down some very strict "rules of engagement" when we were physically fighting. No kicking, no biting, and no touching of the eyes! I remember one Saturday night in the winter, when that sibling love and empathy between Leitchu and me got us both into real trouble. As usual, we were both coughing badly and suffered other childhood maladies. We were bribed to drink *piter mit milech* (hot, boiling milk with lots of butter and sugar in it); it was supposed to cure the terrible wheezing coughs. It was the worst possible treatment. But in addition to the home remedies, both Leah and I had some prescription drugs to take. Mine was as bitter as gall and it looked like it too: a foul tasting and smelling liquid. Leah's on the other hand was a syrupy liquid that tasted real sweet.

That evening, our parents went out somewhere and we were left by ourselves. Leitchu took pity on me that I had to take that bitter medicine every day and she had the good stuff. We decided that blood was thicker than water after all. So we shared, as good loving siblings should. Leah and I each drank half of my full bottle of the bitter medicine, than we shared her bottle of the sweet stuff. We both became sick to our stomachs and heads very quickly. When our parents returned and found the two empty medicine bottles, one of them quickly ran to the druggist on duty and came back with some awful tasting antidote, some kind of crystal, that induced vomiting and cleared our systems out. We were quite sick for a while afterward.

We each had our own friends that came to the house to play. Most of our playing was done on the *mist barg* (trash heap) at the far end of the courtyard. My friends and I would climb on that "mountain" and play "king of the hill" or other such games. We also invented our own games. Sometimes, during school vacations, we would go tree climbing in our neighbor's orchard, stealing apples, pears, and plums. Or we would go to the mountain (the *schlossbarg*) to pick berries and nuts. Often we would disappear right after breakfast and come home for dinner only. Those were still "normal" times when parents didn't have to worry about traffic or other dangers lurking in the streets. We were free to do as we pleased. We, Yolika and I, raised pigeons in cages in the attic. Life was great fun for us while we were too young to understand the apprehension of the grown-ups concerning the terrible war clouds that were beginning to gather over Europe.

This carefree existence came to an abrupt halt around 1936 or 1937. The economic situation had not improved; it actually got worse. Father and some of his friends accepted a lucrative offer from England. It seems that the Orthodox community had a sudden need for several *shochtim*. I was of course too young to know all of the particulars involved in that decision. However, I remember quite well the terrible anxiety we all felt that "here we go again." Father, like grandfather, is leaving us, never to return home again. On the other hand, it made me the man of the house. I was all of eight or nine years old, but I felt duty-bound to become the one to worry that everything is taken care of. In reality, however, mother was quite capable of taking care of all of us.

My playmates were envious of me because father sent us toys and postage stamps from England. I recall the arguments with my friends as to where my father really was. I insisted that he was in England, but they were certain that he was in a place called London. (That's how little we knew about the outside world. We were convinced that Chust was the center of the universe.) We went to the studio of a photographer to take a family portrait to send to father. That was a major and unique event. Normally you went to take a picture for a passport only. (One of those portraits was sent to my grandfather in America, which is how we have a copy of it today.)

As talk of imminent war became more urgent, and when Germany started to make demands on France, Danzig, and Sudetenland, my father decided that his place was with his wife and children. So, after just one year's absence, he returned to us. His colleagues, the ones who originally went with him to England, either remained there or immigrated to America and lost their families in the war. I think that I met one or two of them on the streets of Brooklyn. Father brought us toys and stories of the big world outside. He told us about life in London, of the fog and of the tall buildings. He also brought with him what at the time seemed to us to be very exotic fruits, such as grapefruits, which no one in Chust has ever heard of, let alone actually seen.

One evening, when friends and relatives came to welcome father home, he very expertly and ceremoniously, peeled the "behemoth lemon" and everyone received one section of the very bitter and sour fruit. We did have oranges before but never this strange looking ball. As a matter of fact, since I was always anemic and very skinny because of my poor eating habits, I had the great privilege, on doctor's orders of course, to eat an orange every day. My teacher in *cheder* insisted on peeling that delicacy himself at lunch time and thereafter smell his fingers from time to time to enjoy the precious aroma of the orange that came wrapped in a special wrapper of soft tissue paper with an emblem and the word "Jaffa" imprinted on it. I was also made to take daily doses of cod liver oil and to drink a special kind of expensive red wine to stimulate my appetite. Since my father used to own a bodega, we also had a banana once in a while, which was sliced into thin slices, so that everyone could eat from it. We even had pineapples as a rare treat.

When father came back home, we continued with our special relationship. Only now we also talked about world events and of life in the big cities of the world (he spent a few days in Hamburg, Germany, on his journeys to and from England). We understood each other rather well. I knew exactly what his hopes and expectations were of me and I desperately tried not to disappoint him. I will always remember the broad smile of approval and *nachas sheppen* on my father's face one morning very early, before dawn, when I got up to study the Gemara not in preparation for a test, or for any other reason than just to please him. That was exactly what he expected of me, to learn for the sake of learning. There he stood behind the door separating their bedroom and the living-dining room where I slept, peeking through the sheer curtains. Soon mother, too, joined him.

The holidays were always happy occasions. The fact that mother had a break from her work made us all happy. Pesach, of course, was a very special occasion. We had off from *cheder* the whole month of Nissan. We got very much involved in helping to prepare for this demanding holiday. We helped take the tables from the kitchen outside and carry them near the well in the far end of the backyard and scraped them with knives to remove all crumbs and wash and scrub them with lots of soap and water.

I would also go with my friends to the many hand-matzah bakeries in town to watch the baking of the *matzot*. Sometimes they would even let us do the *reidlen* (puncturing holes in the thin *matzot* with a spur-like little gadget to prevent them from rising before they were baked). All holidays had their own special joys for us. Helping to build a communal *sukkah*, for the use of all the tenants of our courtyard, made me feel very grown up. My most cherished memories of my very early childhood are connected with those rare times when mother didn't have to work. Everyone was relaxed at that time. Mother and Leah were avid readers of novels and magazines. Father and I learned. Yolika was busy with his friends and making plans for getting rich and just being very lovable and cute.

CHEDER AND YESHIVAH DAYS

Like all boys in town, I began my "formal" education at age four. I didn't go to kindergarten, but to a *cheder* (one-room school). This was the beginning of a long string of different *chadarim,* switching every year or so. These schools were strictly for religious training only. There were many choices that our parents had to make. There were many different classes available on the same level. This was the private sector of the Hebrew school system, instead of the city Talmud Torah. Some teachers were strictly teaching early childhood ages, just reading and praying, others specialized in beginning Bible. Others were advanced and taught mostly Talmud. Age was not always the final basis on which the choices were made. The teacher's reputation, the class makeup (who sends their boys to that *cheder*), and the student's ability to absorb what was being learned, as well as the cost, all were variables in the decision making process. Usually the children stayed no more than one year with a particular teacher. If the boy were smart enough, he would be accepted to a higher class with older children.

My career as a student began by learning the *alef beis* in a sing-song manner, the whole class in unison and by heart. We then progressed to begin reading by decoding combinations of consonants and vowels. Then came the actual reading from the *siddur* (prayerbook). This was all accomplished in that first year, at the age of four. I don't recall the names of most of my teachers. I remember the first teacher as being a tall man with a very long beard. The first thing in the morning he would line us up, standing on the long benches, and check to see if we had our *tzitziot* (fringed garment) on and if they were not torn. We then had to put out our hands for inspection to see if they were clean. We recited the basic prayers by heart. The rest of the day was spent drilling, robot-like and by rote memory, the alphabet and the various phonetic combinations. When we could already read from the *siddur*, this too was by rote memorization and never as meaningful prayer. This *cheder* was really nothing more than a one-room storefront, with long tables and benches. It was lit by kerosene or *nafta* lamps (we had to supply the fuel, in turns), a bookshelf and a wood-burning stove (again we took turns in bringing firewood to class during the winter months). Recess was spent by running around in the big yard. Ball playing was forbidden (only *shkotzim*—non-Jewish boys—play ball).

A series of other teachers and other *chadarim* followed in rapid succession. Some of the teachers were cruel and beat the little kids with actual force. Many children came home with bruises and black and blue marks all over their bodies. Luckily, my mother, bless her soul, loved us too much and was too progressive to abandon us to the questionable mercies of the teachers. She made it very clear to every new teacher that they must keep their hands and sticks off of us. It was obvious that she meant it. Once I came home with signs of physical abuse by the teacher. Mother sent word to him the same day that I would be transferring out to another *cheder* the next day. The very same evening the poor man came to the house and begged to be forgiven. Since we were among the very few parents who actually paid their tuition on time and since I happened to be a very good student, it was important for him that I return to his *cheder*. After some lecturing, I was permitted to go back to him. He never again touched me. There were stories of some teachers spanking little boys on their bare behinds.

The day at *cheder* would begin very early in the morning. We would walk there by ourselves and carry our lunch, books, and the occasional supply of fuel. Often, some of our non-Jewish neighbors would wait for us and attack us with fists or rocks. One of my front, permanent upper teeth was lost to one of those rocks. For the most part our only defense was to try to outrun them. In the winter, we walked through high snow and very cold temperatures. The frozen snow would grunt under our high shoes. At age eight or nine, we walked to *cheder* before dawn, with candle-burning lanterns in hand, in the pitch dark and abandoned streets.

Going to *cheder* and learning Torah became the only real and meaningful purpose of growing up. Alas, both Czech and, later on, Hungarian law demanded compulsory attendance in public school. We reluctantly had to divide the day between the two systems. Under the democratic regime of Czechoslovakia, there were three separate, recognized, and autonomous public school systems in town: Czech, Ruthenian, and Hungarian. Most of my friends and I preferred the Czech schools. We walked between home, *cheder*, and school a couple of times during the day. Our elementary school building was in the Colonia, the Czech quarter of town where most of the civil servants lived. We participated in all extracurricular activities together with the non-Jewish kids. The school was a beautiful building with a gym, arts and crafts shop, and music classes. There was never a question as to which of the two schools was more important. Secular education held no interest at all to most of us. It was an evil imposed on us, just like the Greeks and their Hellenistic Jews did during the Chanukah events of history. We never cared about grades or about doing homework. After all this was "goyish" culture, not worthy of our time or effort. I became a very good *cheder yingel* but a very bad secular school student.

After going through several teachers over many years, I became eligible, at age eight or nine, to enter the truly elitist and most prestigious class of Reb Shea Farkash. It was the dream and the highest aspiration of every boy in town to reach this level. When you were accepted by Reb Shea, it meant that you "earned your stripes." It was as high as you could go in the *cheder* world in our town. From there it was an easy jump to the yeshivah (rabbinic seminary) world.

Reb Shea was an unusual human being. He respected his pupils as responsible young men and we responded in kind. We truly looked forward to go to his class. We didn't mind the long hours, late into the night, sitting and absorbing what he taught us. He was an educator *par excellence*, a natural-born teacher who understood children and their individual modes of learning. The fact that he lived far away from the center of town didn't stop most of us from gathering around him, voluntarily, on Shabbat afternoons, sitting in his vineyard at the back of his house and learning from him whatever subject he wanted to discuss with us. I can truly say that his influence was deep and everlasting on all of us. My friend and classmate Rabbi Yisroel Dovid Neuwohner, like myself, became a very successful teacher and principal (in Los Angeles). We have always agreed that, without really trying or even being conscious of it, we both have owed our success as educators to Reb Shea. We always remembered him with great love and appreciation and we always strived to emulate him as our role model of a true educator.

The fact that I love learning and teaching, and enjoy hearing that I have a good way of explaining complex ideas—I owe it all to his inspiration. During the three years that I had the merit to be his student, I managed to accumulate a great portion, if not most, of my current knowledge of intricate and subtle ways of the Talmud, Jewish law, and history.

His *cheder* could hold only twenty-three chairs around the two tables in his one-room school, and twenty-three boys were the only lucky ones to be accommodated. One could offer him all the money in the world but that still could not get your son admitted into his class if he was not a serious student or if the twenty-three seats were filled. Those of us who did get in realized how lucky we were and we did everything to earn our place. Reb Shea had a large family. Alas, he did not (nor any one of his large family) come back from Auschwitz. What a loss to all of his past and potential students.

My Bar Mitzvah celebration also marked the approaching passing of my *cheder* years and the beginning of my yeshivah days. Unlike what has become the custom of late to make the Bar Mitzvah celebration a rehearsal for the wedding, in our circles and times, it was not a big deal at all. No one studied to read the Torah. There were no catered affairs either. To me the occasion was marked by two events. One, for the very first time in my life I got a tailored suit with long pants. Until then, every Pesach my brother and I had new tailor-made suits, with short pants only. This, then, was the right of passage.

On a Thursday, the 4th day of Tamuz, which was the actual day of my thirteenth birthday by the Jewish calendar, I began to put on *tefilin*. My father brought to *shul* a bottle of whiskey and cake to drink a *lechayim*. On that day I was called up to the Torah for the first time in my life.

In the afternoon of that Shabbat, a lot of my relatives, friends, and neighbors were invited to our home. The tables were laden with light food and drinks. Then came the second event. For about forty-five minutes I recited a *pilpul* (a complex talmudic analysis). Of course, it was Reb Shea Farkash who helped me develop the ideas I expressed. For that occasion a twenty-five liter keg of beer was opened in the kitchen. Since nobody had much experience with how to go about opening such a keg, it literally popped its cork like a geyser under pressure. The stain it made on the ceiling would not disappear even after many re-paintings.

My thirteenth year was a true test of my mettle. The time had come for me to leave the shelter of my home and travel to another city to study in a yeshivah. The fact that Chust had one of the most prestigious *yeshivot* didn't do me any good for two reasons. First, I couldn't attend since the *rosh hayeshivah*, the official Rav of the *kehilah,* was boycotted by the Satmar Hasidim. Second, every boy who was serious about learning just had to go out of town in order "to grow up" and study earnestly, without the interruptions of home life. All boys had to face up to this reality one day. My day had now arrived.

Luckily, my first traumatic experience at being a full-fledged *yeshivah bochur* was tempered by the fact that my parents sent me to the nearest available town with a yeshivah, Teich. It was my father's birthplace and we had many relatives still living there. Since both of my paternal grandparents were no longer alive, I was put up in *quartir* (rooming), in their house, where only my aunt Etya lived alone. My close friend and classmate from infancy shared the spare bedroom with me. (Today he is a retired lieutenant colonel from the Israel Defense Forces. When I first came to Israel on a visit in 1954, I naturally went to visit him at his command post. He was then a captain. I couldn't believe my eyes. In his office at the military post on a shelf were a *Shas* (Talmud set) and other *sefarim.* He was a regular army commander of a combat unit, not in the chaplaincy, but found time to learn—Reb Shea's inspiration, no doubt. He still lives in Israel where he and his wife are raising a fine family.)

We studied very hard and long hours. We also had *essen teig* (eating days). There is no way to describe accurately the emotions, the humiliation, and sometimes the actual starvation, that this practice brought with it. It meant that every *bochur* (yeshivah student) ate each day of the week in a different home. Some homes treated you nicely, while in others you ate in the kitchen with the servants. In some homes the food was plentiful while in others it was barely enough to survive. We learned quickly that like Joseph in Egypt it was wise to gather the food of the good days and store them up for the lean days. Every evening, we emptied out our pockets and stored away the day's haul. I had minimal problems only, since most of my "days" were either with relatives or with friends of the family.

Still, on Sundays in particular, I was terribly embarrassed. I ate with the Berger family. They were my father's cousins and were extremely nice to me. However, they had a daughter just about my age and I felt terribly self-conscious. One day catastrophe struck. My pants split at the seam as I bent down to pick up a spoon that fell out of my shaky hand. I thought that the earth would split open and let me hide there. Instead, I quickly ran out of the house in a panic. About halfway out of the courtyard, I heard the voice of that girl calling after me. I kept on going. She came running after me with my lunch in a paper bag (what I failed to finish in the house before I fled). I ran all the way back to my room where I took out my sewing kit. (Yes, I learned how to sew on buttons, to mend socks, as well as to wash and iron my shirts and pants. This was part of the reason for going away to yeshivah rather than to staying in town. You had to learn how to take care of yourself and of your needs.)

The only big problems I encountered revolved around my terrible eating habits. Many times, when I didn't like what was served, I waited until no one was looking and wrapped the food in a napkin and put it in my pocket to throw it away when I left. Sometimes, especially with soups and such, I would put the plate on the chair and move the chair under the table and leave in a hurry. *Essen teig* did not cure my fussiness about what I would eat. Only after Auschwitz did I finally begin to change some of this terrible pattern. Just some. For I am still a very big problem to my wife and especially to our hosts whenever we are invited for lunch or dinner. By now, most of our friends know my problem and some of them would actually call beforehand to inquire if I would eat a particular dish or not.

I spent two years in Teich. It was now time to move on to a more intensive yeshivah. For some reason, about seven or eight of my cousins chose to travel to a very small village in Hungary as the best place to learn. The village was called Nir Hadasz. It is between the towns of Nir Bator and Mateszalka. The Jewish population in the village did not exceed twenty-five families out of a total population of perhaps 100 families. Yet the yeshivah accommodated over seventy boys. It was chosen perhaps because of the small size of the village, with obviously nothing else to do but sit in *beis medrish* from dawn till late night and study.

The *rosh hayeshivah* (dean) was a great scholar. Since there were not enough Jewish homes to accommodate all of the boys with *essen teig*, the rebetzin and her daughters personally cooked all the meals for the entire yeshivah! We rented sleeping space from the few Jewish families in the village. About ten of us stayed with the Pava family. Ten cots in one relatively small room! There were no wooden floors and no electricity. There were three over-sized, wrestler-type boys in that family. They were our bodyguards and protected us from the fists and the stones of the villagers who had no other entertainment available to them than to look for Jewish boys to beat up. Here I learned besides the required lessons how to roll my own cigarettes and how to smoke them without choking.

Since there was no local community to speak of that could even remotely provide the financial support for the yeshivah and for the feeding of seventy young men, the *rosh hayeshivah* relied heavily on outside support. The parents, even those few who could afford it, could not pay the full cost, and most of the boys came from poor families anyway.

While learning in Hadasz, I traveled with the whole yeshivah to the town of Kalev to participate in the prayers in the cave at the grave of the famous Kalever Rebbe (he composed very famous Hasidic songs in Hungarian, such as "*Sol a Kakash Mar*"). There I met for the first time and received the blessings of Reb Sholem Leizer Halbershtam, the Ratzferder Rebbe. He was in his eighties. He was the youngest son of Reb Chayim Sanzer.

That same year, our yeshivah dean picked ten of his students and we traveled to Budapest to spend a Shabbat with the Alter Belzer Rebbe, Reb Ahrele Rokeach, who escaped the Nazis from Poland and spent several months recuperating in Budapest before settling in what was then Palestine. My father, who at this time was traveling regularly to Budapest to buy and sell textiles in wholesale, stayed over for Shabbat, instead of going home on Thursday, as usual. It was a real treat for me. The big capital city was alluring—so many wonders to see. Elevators and escalators, big stores, the zoo and the amusement parks... Father took me to eat in some very nice restaurants. And of course there was the spiritual experience of sitting the entire Shabbat in the same room with the Belzer Rebbe and watching him every minute of the day and night. After receiving the Rebbe's blessings, we returned to Hadasz. What an experience!

Since all my years of *cheder* and yeshivah until 1944 were spent exclusively in Hasidic surroundings, all of our time was spent on the study of Chumash-Rashi, Talmud, *Shulchan Aruch,* and Mussar (ethics). The study of Navi (the Prophets and Scriptures), Rambam, Hebrew, history, and literature were strictly forbidden. They could lead a person to become an *apikores* (heretic)! They may even lead to further study of philosophy and other secular studies on a high school or even college level. They could even lead to Zionism, G-d forbid! Until after my auto-emancipation, after the war, I had no knowledge of these treasures of Judaic studies.

1938–1944

While I was naively enjoying life in *cheder* and playing with my friends, we were, for the most part, completely oblivious to what was going on in the world outside our little center of the Earth, Chust. The Czech government was very good to the Jews. There was no reason for us not to believe that we would forever live in peace and tranquility, and enjoy our families and friends. Nothing could have been further removed from reality.

Dark clouds of war were gathering over all of Europe. We, the kids, had very little insight into what was really going on. We only heard new, strange words being uttered that had no meaning at all to us. Anschluss, Dolfus, Zeisenquart, and Schushnick in Austria. Sudetengebit, Minchen, Chamberlain, Henlein, appeasement, etc., in Czechoslovakia. Hitler, Ribentrop, and Goring in Germany. Mussolini, Graf Ciano, and Abesinia in Italy. The Maginot Line, Marshal Petain, Daladier, Alsace-Loraine, the Saar and Ruhr Gebit, and the Oder-Neisse Line, Maginot line, in France. The Corridor to Danzig in Poland. The border war between Poland and Czechoslovakia over a place called Tczeshin, etc. All of these names and places were whispered in heated and animated discussions among the grown-ups, but had no meaning at all to us. We could sense the concern and the deep apprehension with which these ominous names and words were spoken, but we had no idea of why or how any of these far away places should be any of our concerns. We had more important things to worry about... We lived in a fool's paradise....

How wrong we were! Some time in 1938–39, we realized that Czechoslovakia was in trouble. The Ruthenians were openly talking of separating from Czechoslovakia and set up their own independent state. Suddenly, we were transferred to the Ruthenian (Ukrainian) public school system, as the Czechs were trying to appease the locals. We learned to read, speak, and write Ukrainian (the Cyrillic Azbuka, in place of the Latin alphabet). Even though this lasted for one year only, I can still read and understand some of it.

Around Rosh Hashanah (October 1938) the Czech army fully mobilized. Every able-bodied man up to age sixty was put in uniform and began training in the disciplines of the military. My father, too, was put into a brand new uniform. He was a dashing figure in it with his bayonet, gas mask, and canteen hanging from his belt. Soldiers were housed in school buildings. We were allowed to visit him there. The Czechs were determined to stand up and fight the Germans, Italians, and Hungarians for their twenty-year-old Republic. However (as I learned later from reading some of the history of World War II), they soon realized that they were betrayed by all of their allies and that it would be suicide to try to fight the Germans alone. After President Eduard Benes (Thomas Masaryk, the great humanitarian and real democratic Father of the Czech Republic, was no longer alive at this time) returned in defeat from Munich, abandoned by the British and French politicians, whose empty promises would not stand the light of day, and by their Brother Russian Slavs, who claimed that they could not get permission from Poland to come to the aid of the Czechs, the mobilized army was sent home. The Czech civil servants began packing to move back to the Czech lands of Bohemia and Moravia. They sold most of their belongings at a fraction of their cost or true value. We bought some expensive pieces of furniture from them. It was a very sad time for everyone. We loved the Czechs. We had no idea what would come after they left us. We were sad to see them leave in retreat. They were miserably betrayed by everyone. A new Czech president, Hacha, collaborated with the Nazis.

In the meantime, the local Ruthenian-Ukrainians organized themselves into paramilitary units and into a political aspirant to govern after the Czechs left. Their rag-tag army of peasants and thieves became the feared terrorist "Sichackes." They terrorized the hapless Czechs to induce them to leave everything behind and leave in a hurry. Their leader, Voloshin, a Pravoslavny (Russian Orthodox) priest and a well-known anti-Semite and Jew-baiter, instigated and riled up his followers with his inflammatory preaching, that the Jews are the Czech's allies and partners in the exploitation of the poor peasants. The Sichackes began putting together a list of prominent Jews to be executed publicly after the Czechs would leave and they would take over. We found out about the existence of that list and all the wealthy and prominent Jews on it, and they all began to make plans to escape as soon as they would be able to. But it never came to that stage.

In March 1939, as the Czechs were beginning their withdrawal, with trucks and train loads of soldiers with their weapons, the Sichackes could not contain themselves any longer. They attacked the Czechs with firearms and with sickles and axes. The Czechs fought a rear-guard battle for several days. Father Voloshin declared the independent state of Karpatska-Ukraina (Ruthenia) with Chust as its capital.

In the meantime, perhaps without the Sichackes' knowledge, the Germans decided to dismember all of Czechoslovakia. The Sudetenland was formally annexed to Germany. Slovakia was granted "independence," as a full German satellite nation of course, with the rabid anti-Semitic Monsignor Tisso as president. Slovakia immediately became a hell on Earth for the nearly one hundred thousand Jews who lived and thrived there under the federated republic with Czechia. (This priest, Tisso, was later captured by the Allied forces in Germany, tried as a war criminal, and publicly hanged after the war.)

The Germans awarded Carpatho-Russ (Ruthenia) to their Axis partner, the Hungarians. The Sichackes hoped to create and proclaim their own state as a fait accompli before the Czechs completely moved out. A fierce battle broke out between the Ukrainians and the Czechs in the streets of Chust. We, the kids, loved it. We had been playing soldiers with broom handles ever since we heard the rumors of the approaching war. We were going to be ready. We especially loved the fact that school and *cheder* were closed, because it was too dangerous to venture out on the streets. We watched with fascination as the Sichackes with their yellow and blue national colors and armbands, with rifles, machine guns, and hand grenades, were shooting at the Czechs and at everything else that was moving in the street. I remember the big blast we heard when a rifle grenade was shot at the big *shul*, almost across the street from us. We huddled at the gate of our courtyard to watch the battle and get a first hand, blow-by-blow explanation of what was being fired and by whom from one of our neighbors who was recently released from the Czech army as a sergeant. It was really exciting stuff for us. We felt sorry only for the poor horses that were hitched to the wagons laden with textiles and other goods to be sold on the big market day on Wednesday. They trembled and made an effort to bolt every time a shot was fired. All grown-ups scurried around in the attics, closets, and basements to find some pieces of cloth, from old shirts, dresses, and such, from which to fashion makeshift yellow and blue flags to display as a sign of loyalty to the new rulers of the land, the Ukrainian Sichackes.

The street battles ended at last on Tuesday late afternoon. We were still officially Czech citizens at that time. However, when we woke up on Wednesday morning, we found out that the last of the Czech army had left overnight and that we were now the proud and loyal citizens of the newest state on Earth, called Zapadna Ukraina (Western Ukraine). A government was formed with Voloshin as the president. The Corona Hotel became the Nazi German Embassy and displayed a huge German flag with a swastika. This was the very first time that we ever saw that dreaded and hateful emblem of evil incarnate. We were terrified of what they would now do to us. We cried our eyes out (the grown-ups, that is, not us kids; to us it was still all fun and games as usual). The Ukrainian State had printed proclamations posted all over town to notify us that we were now under their rule and that Chust was now the capital city of the new state. They had already printed new paper currency that would be exchanged for the Czech cronas. They even had a rubber stamp to superimpose on the leftover Czech postage stamps. (These items later became much sought-after collector's items of enormous value.) It was a time for fasting and prayers for the entire adult community.

On Thursday, rumors began making the rounds that there was fighting going on not far from town. Something was in the air. Suddenly, we saw the Sichackes running in all directions. We had no idea what was happening, but fewer and fewer Ukrainians with the armbands were seen in the center of town. Around 4–5 P.M. that same Thursday we became the proud and loyal citizens of Hungary! Once again, the closets, attics, and cellars were searched to find some cloth with the right combination of the patriotic colors to be hoisted on the rooftops or at least made into an armband or even a tiny strip to fit into a lapel buttonhole. It was not easy, but a lot of people, especially the Jews, found the coveted combinations of red, white, and green. For the Jews it was a double celebration.

First, the Jews greeted the Hungarian army as genuine liberators, after what was certain to have been a bloodbath and outright massacre, had the Ukrainians stayed in power long enough and carried out their planned pogroms against the Jews. Second, most Jews were brought up under the benign rule of Emperor Franz Joseph of the Austro-Hungarian Empire, attended Hungarian schools, and spoke the language fluently. For most of our parents it was a real liberation. Most of the older generation never had managed to learn either the Czech or the Ukrainian languages. Neither of my parents, who were both born and raised among the majority Ruthenians, and had lived for twenty years under the Czechs, had ever bothered to try and learn the history or the culture of those two nations. They were and remained, at least in their hearts and minds, Hungarians by culture. So it was no wonder that as many Jews as could make it came out to the main square in front of the big *shul* to warmly and genuinely greet the "invading" Hungarian army with food and drink and pleasant conversation.

That's how it came about that within three consecutive days we were citizens of three different states. I don't think that anyone else can boast of a similar record. We had to adjust, once again, to a new school system and, for us, a new language and new rules. I have no idea to this day of what had actually happened that made the Germans turn the Hungarians against the Ukrainians in the span of only two days. All I know is that for us it was nothing short of miraculous. The German flag with its dreadful swastika disappeared from the Corona Hotel and we had a breather. Or so we thought....

The Hungarians were Axis partners with the Germans. They too were on the march to re-establish the glorious Austro-Hungarian Empire of before 1918. Hitler gave them parts of Rumania and parts of Yugoslavia that were once integral parts of the Empire. But there was a price to be paid for all of these gifts. And as is usually the case, we the Jews, had to pay it. After only two to three years of relative tranquility, the Germans began planning the "Final Solution" to the Jewish problem and did not leave us out of their murderous scheme.

Special anti-Jewish laws began to be proclaimed from time to time by the town crier and his drum and by posted notices. Some stores owned by Jews were taken away and given to Hungarians. Kosher meat was outlawed. Jews could no longer hold public office. Jewish children could no longer attend public schools. Jewish doctors could not treat non-Jewish patients; Jews could not use the sidewalks if a non-Jew came toward them. Soon we were ordered to sew on yellow swatches (I can't recall now if they had to be in the form of a Star of David) on our clothes. The soldiers would have "sport" by forcefully shaving off the beards of very pious Jews who were grabbed on the streets. Many Jews decided to shave off their beards themselves rather then become victimized by the soldiers. Father was among them. He just wasn't the same dashing figure without his distinguished looking beard. Many young men were drafted into forced labor paramilitary battalions (*munkaszolgálat*). They wore civilian clothes with yellow armbands and regular army caps. They were commanded by regular military officers, under regular military rule, except that they did not have weapons and were used for hard labor, attached to military units. They dug and cleaned the latrines, chopped the firewood, scrubbed the cooking pots and pans for the soldiers, and so on. A few hundred of them were billeted temporarily in the Dunkel furniture factory in Chust, for short training periods.

Parallel to these *munkaszolgálat* battalions, and even prior to this time, the Hungarians also had a youth organization called the Leventes. This was somewhat like a combination of Boy Scouts and R.O.T.C. Every boy, regardless of his religion, had to join this organization. We wore military-like uniforms and met once a week, after school, for diversified activities and paramilitary weapons drills with wooden, look-a-like rifles, and lectures on civic and community service. We were very eager to reach the age of about ten or eleven, when we would become eligible to join the Leventes. As soon as the special anti-Jewish laws were proclaimed and the *munkaszolgálat* for the grown-ups were established the same thing happened to us, the Leventes. We had to give up the uniforms and the wooden rifles. All we had left were the military caps and yellow armbands. We became errand boys and clean-up crews for the non-Jewish Leventes and to the regular army officers and noncoms who were in charge of this youth organization.

Some of these adult work battalions were sent to the fighting fronts of the Ukraine and Russia as well as to the former Yugoslav and Rumanian lands. Many died of frost and starvation. Some were shot by the Germans and their willing allies (Hungarians, Serbs, Croats, Rumanians, Ukrainians, etc.). Others eventually wound up in Auschwitz and in other concentration camps. Some deserted their units and joined the "partisans" in the forests, fighting a resistance war against the Germans.

Those proclamations and regulations came in intervals, not all at once. In 1941 many Jews who could not prove Hungarian citizenship were forced to leave the country or to try and obtain such citizenship (usually by forgery or by bribery).

Around Tisha B'Av 1941 many of the Jews who had no Hungarian citizenship papers were rounded up by the Kakashes (the civilian police with the rooster feathers in their hats; *kakash* = rooster) and the dreaded Hatarvadasz, (brutal border-police units), together with all of their families, put into cattle cars, and forcefully deported. Most of them were from the villages and from the mountain communities. We, therefore, didn't know many of them personally (I found out later, after the war, that my dearest aunt, Mime Sheindel, and her family were among the deportees), and we fooled ourselves into believing that they were removed from the sensitive areas near the border with Poland, even though Poland was already long ago subdued by the Blitzkrieg and there was no fear of disloyal Jews living near that border. We told ourselves that they were re-settled somewhere inside Hungary.

Only much later did we find out that they were taken across the border into what once was Poland, and around the towns of Tlust, Kolomei, and Kamenetz-Podolsk, they were forced to dig long trenches. They were lined up along those ravines and methodically machine-gunned and buried by the SS murderers in those trenches. We found all of that out from a handful of less than ten survivors who found their way back to Chust and told us of what had happened. We refused to believe those stories. When the Hungarian authorities found out about people harboring such refugees, they jailed those who gave them shelter or food.

Life still went on. We were still learning in the *yeshivot* and we still traveled to the Satmarer Rebbe for some holidays. I was even taken to Sighet to attend the wedding of Chanele, the daughter of the "Atzei Chayim" (the Chief Rabbi of Sighet). There I met the Ratzferder Rebbe for the second time and received his blessings.

To digress a little... When the German army overran Poland, a large part of the Polish army fled to Hungary. They came by trucks, by horse-drawn wagons, on horseback, on motorcycles, and on bicycles—a real rag-tag army. Among them were many Jews. I even remember a rabbi among them, who served as chaplain in that army. They remained "parked" on the main road in town, in complete military formations, for many days. We brought food for those who needed kosher food from the *kehilah*-sponsored free kitchen. They began, little by little, to desert their units, acquire false identities, and settle in Hungary, at least temporarily. The bulk of that army, a few thousand of them, were eventually disarmed by the Hungarians and put into internment camps. Some of the Jews among them later on wound up in concentration camps too.

In Slovakia, under the Fascist rule of Father Tisso and his bullies, the "Iron Guards," the Jews immediately felt the heavy fist of the Nazi oppression. Jews were in the concentration camps as soon as Germans established them. In fact many Jews formed the forced labor that built several of the most infamous camps. Some tried desperately to send warnings in clandestine messages to their relatives in Hungary to flee for their lives while they could still do so. This was as early as 1940. But nobody believed them. Some claimed that it was all just hysteria. They chose to believe that the Hungarians were trying to cause panic among the Jews so they could confiscate their properties after they fled and left everything behind. These baseless rationalizations by the majority of the Jews helped convince them that all the rumors were false and that nothing but the usual persecutions would be visited upon them. After all, they were loyal Hungarian citizens, and their patron, Horthy Miklos, the Chancellor of Hungary, was married to a half-Jewish woman! He would certainly protect them from harm.

Around this time, my father and I went on one of our regular visits to Satmar we discussed with the Rebbe the fact that my father was offered a certificate to make *aliyah* to Palestine, with his entire family. He was offered that prized and cherished award for his very active role in the Poalei Agudat Yisrael organization. The Rebbe strongly advised father against doing such a thing. *Aliyah* was for the despised Zionists only! And if the Rebbe said "no," it meant NO!

This was the terrible price we all paid for the blind faith that an otherwise clever man, such as our father surely was, put in the super-human infallibility of another human being made of flesh and blood, rather than thinking and making decisions for himself. I feel very sorry for my father realizing, albeit much too late, that his trust was misguided. What torture of guilt he must have suffered! Till this day, I am amazed at the thousands of smart Jews and Gentiles too who still put their faith and fate into the hands of other, untrained, unproven, and unprofessional humans. It took me many hundreds of hours of therapy, after the war, to free myself ever so slowly and haltingly at first from the unquestioned "truth" that the Rebbe is the "Guardian Angel" of his flock. I am convinced now that no one has the right to take the responsibility on himself to make life or death decisions for another, sane human being.

The bitter irony of fate that I have to live with is the fact that this same Satmarer Rebbe saved himself, as one of the refugees on the notorious Kastner train, that went from Bergen-Belsen to Palestine. For him Palestine was good enough to save his life, but not for his faithful followers.

By the beginning of 1943, the oppression against the Jews became intolerable. By now most of the Jewish-owned stores and shops were already confiscated and given over to anyone who applied for them, as long as they were not Jewish. Food shortages were common for everyone, but the Jews were the very last ones on the list for whatever was available. I no longer could travel away from home to learn in a yeshivah. Very reluctantly and with real trepidation, my father consented to allow me to attend the local, very famous yeshivah. I am sure he realized that these were extraordinary times and that the Rebbe's decree against the Chuster Rav, Reb Shea, no longer had the same force as in more normal times. This was the time also when I became my father's *chavrusa* (study partner) every morning and evening in the Atzei Chaim Beis Medrish, where we studied together.

The war was at its height. We heard news, second- and third-hand, that the Germans were on the march. We knew that France and the rest of Western Europe were occupied. We were also aware that Bohemia and Moravia, the remnants of the only true democracy of Central Europe, were now under German occupation as a "protectorate."

The Germans Come to Town

The Hungarian fascists, the Nyilash Party (the "Arrow-cross" hoodlums), were gaining more power every day. Horthy was losing favor with the Fuhrer, perhaps because of his reluctance to cooperate fully and willingly with Adolf Eichmann in the liquidation of Hungarian Jewry. Of course, we had no knowledge of what was really going on. Jews were not permitted to own or even to listen to a radio. We heard rumors that Horthy's eldest son, Istvan, a fighter pilot in the Hungarian air force, had mysteriously crashed. Everyone was fully convinced that he was shot down by the Germans because of his views that were too liberal for the Nyilashes. Horthy was deposed and replaced by Szalosy, a Nyilash puppet of the Germans. Eventually Horthy wound up in a German concentration camp too. He survived and was last seen by some Hungarian Jews in a displaced persons camp. Rumors were still reaching the grown-ups, which we, the kids, could not help but pick up, about the fate of the Jews of Germany, Slovakia, and Poland. As usual, it was easier to live with denial than to be forced to deal with reality. Not that reality offered any alternatives of possible action or escape.

Passover 1944 began in the usual way, except that there was a shortage of *matzot*, eggs, and potatoes, the mainstays of the holiday staples. The first Seder father conducted as best he could. The only real problem was the food shortage.

The shock of our lives arrived on the morning after. Without any warning, the German army marched into town and took over as an occupying force. Our parents' bedroom, because it had a separate entrance from the outside, was requisitioned as a billet for two German Wermacht (regular army) officers. The second Seder was conducted in a whisper, in the kitchen. No salt water was needed to remind us of the tears, nor any *maror* to remind us of the bitter times that our forefathers had endured in Egypt so long ago. We suddenly realized that our turn too had arrived. But for what? We had no concrete ideas, only very bad premonitions. That night, we heard for the first time for real, rather than just as a practice, the air raid warning sirens. The German officers, our new next-door neighbors (literally next door), the very genial and friendly officers, reassured us that there were no enemy planes in the sky. As we all waited outside for the all-clear signal, the people engaged the officers in friendly chitchat. They told us of their families back home and how much they missed them. They also confided that they were tired and exhausted of the long war, and they would much rather be at home and go on with their lives. We were quickly convinced that the Germans are not such bad people after all!

That second Seder night, my father turned to me and asked: "Did you ever pay attention to the special way that I always intone the Hebrew word *shene'emar* during the recitation of the Haggadah? I don't know what will happen to us, but if you survive the war, I want you to promise me that you will continue saying it in the same manner. This is the way my father learned it from his father. This has been a family tradition for many generations!" Of course, I could not completely comprehend why he was telling me this at that time, but the solemnity of the words and the manner in which they were spoken told me that he knew something about our futures that we were too young to have figured out for ourselves. I did, of course, promise him and burst out crying uncontrollably.

It was more like Tisha B'Av (the national day of mourning for the destruction of the Holy Temple in Jerusalem) than Pesach. It was more Lamentation than Haggadah. Not that the word *shene'emar* has any special, overt, or hidden meaning. It is the intonation of it that formed the basis of father's request. He didn't survive. And I kept my solemn promise to him ever since then. My two sons have also received the word and accepted the duty to carry on the family tradition. Oh, how I wish that I could somehow reassure my dear father that we have not forgotten! The tradition lives on. What a pity that he could not have lived long enough to see his grandchildren follow in his footsteps. And perhaps even his great-grandchildren will too.

Within the next few days, things began to move in rapid order. The Gestapo arrested the city's Chief Rabbi and about forty to fifty of the leading Jewish personalities as hostages. They were locked up in our precious Atzei Chaim Beis Medrish. The Beis Hamedrish became a torture camp. We heard of terrible outcries, moaning, and groaning coming out of the *shul*. Reb Menashe Neuwohner was among those suffering physically and emotionally in the very place where for so many years he had led us in the High Holiday prayers. All the Torah scrolls were torn up and desecrated. The Gestapo also confiscated their properties and moneys. They appointed a "Judenrat," a Jewish council of their own choosing to collaborate with them and to act as a conduit for their decrees. They freed the rabbi and made him personally responsible to keep the people under control. All the new orders and rules from the Gestapo came via the Judenrat.

LIFE IN THE GHETTO

After the first few days of the German takeover, the Gestapo, accompanied by the Hungarian "Hatarvadasz" (border police), came to each Jewish home in town and gave them a few minutes to pack up their essential belongings and be ready to move into the Ghetto, which was set up on a few streets of the town and surrounded by a barbed wire fence. We had already previously buried most of our possessions in the cellar under the Belzer Klaus in our courtyard. We dug a huge hole, put a metal tub in the hole, and filled it up with everything we had of real value as soon as we heard of the Ghetto being set up.

At that time, I remember a great deal of arguments and screaming going on in our town. Some high school students of the Hebrew, Zionistic school and members of some youth organizations in town wanted to join their friends to escape into the mountains and organize themselves into "partisan" units to fight the Germans. Others dreamed of finding a way to reach the ocean and immigrate to Palestine. Some of them even had acquired handguns. They were all driven by a desperate desire to live and to be of some help to the rest of us. However, most of the adults, father among them, insisted that no matter what awaits us in the future, we must all stay together as a community and that families must stay together if they are to have any future at all. They strongly believed that all of this trouble would soon pass, as did all the other persecutions throughout our long history. A few of the young people did not pay attention to the advice of their elders. They left town. Some succeeded to escape the ultimate fate of their parents. Others perished while trying.

Soon our turn came to be kicked out of our home and to move into the Ghetto. We all took some bundles on our shoulders, *a la* the Exodus from Egypt, and followed the Gestapo on the march toward one of the designated areas. All of the non-Jewish population of Chust, without noticeable exceptions, lined the streets and denigrated us with shouts of obscenities and spit. We went in long lines, some with babies in their arms, others with carriages packed with some food, blankets, and other small household items, and cried all the way. Luckily, the street where our grandmother lived, the Reita Gass, was included within one of the fenced-in Ghetto sections. There were two or three such Ghetto areas in town. They were not all in the same areas, and there was no way to visit or otherwise communicate between them.

The Ghetto consisted primarily of a few streets, with the dividing fences between the various courtyards removed, to create one large, easily controllable section. High fences were erected around each one of those sections, and the Hungarian border patrol policemen guarded the perimeters and the entrances against escape or contact of any kind with the outside world. Only burial parties were allowed to leave the Ghetto, under heavy guard. Some members of the Judenrat, and other essentially needed persons, were permitted to leave the Ghetto for part of the day, under guard. The hostages kept in the Atzei Chaim Beis Medrish were the guarantors against any attempt of escape or civil disobedience. From time to time, we heard of some young people, primarily members of Zionist youth movements, who managed to either bribe their way or slip out at night, with false, Aryan identity papers, and go to Budapest and from there to the port of Constansa in Rumania, and board some of the boats that were headed for Palestine, without the authorities finding out about them. Once again, Leitchu was offered the chance to escape with one of those Mizrachi groups, and once again father insisted that we remain together and face whatever the future holds for us, as a family.

We found out, after the war was over, that many of those who finally made good their escape from the Ghetto and boarded the boats, on their way to freedom in Palestine, never made it. Some were shot out of the seas either by the Germans or by the British navy who enforced the White Paper against Jewish immigration into Palestine, as they had promised the Arabs to do. *The Patria* was one of those unlucky, leaky little boats that were sunk. One of our neighbors, who lived in our courtyard, Nuta Miller, was among those who had died on the high seas on his way to the Promised Land. However, my cousin Leiby (Yehudah) Zelkowitz did make it to the shores of Palestine. Others hid in the thick forests of the high Carpathian Mountains and joined the resistance groups. Some just stayed in Budapest, with false papers, until the war was over.

While the Hungarians were responsible for the outside security, it was the Gestapo and the Judenrat that dealt with internal order and security. Often we were ordered to stand at attention outside the buildings, to be inspected by some very high-ranking SS and Gestapo officers who came to "visit" us.

Once inside the walls of the Ghetto, we were allowed to find our own accommodations. Naturally, our family and most of our other relatives settled in with our grandmother. We were literally like sardines in a can. We slept tightly packed on the floors of her one-and-a-half room apartment. I don't remember exactly how many we were, but we were at least twenty or more people jammed and cramped in together. The days passed with attempts to scrounge up food and with speculations and rumors as to what the Germans had in mind for us. We deceived ourselves into thinking that the war would soon be over and we would return home. Alas, it was not to be thus.

After only a few weeks, about six or so, we heard that one of the Ghetto sections was evacuated. We had no idea where they were taken, or if it was true at all. Rumors were all the "concrete" news we had. The one rumor we liked best was that we would be taken and relocated into the interior territories of Hungary, away from the mountains, because the Russians were on the offensive and may soon reach the Carpathian region. We would all be put into internment camps to work and help protect the Motherland.

On a Thursday morning in June, just before the holiday of Shavuot, we were told to pack up our essential belongings and be ready to move out of the Ghetto. Leitchu was seventeen, I was just two months away from my sixteenth birthday, and Yolika had just become a Bar Mitzvah a few months earlier. We were in total darkness as to what was going on. We were unaware of what was being planned for us. Nor did I personally worry too much about the situation. I had complete confidence in my parents' abilities to protect us from any harm. And, after all, we were all fine Hasidic, observant, and pious Jews; surely the Rebbe would have warned us if something bad were to going to happen to us. He would deflect the bad decrees of our enemies. And of course Hashem knew that we were studying Torah and praying to Him day and night; He certainly would look after us! So I just went about the business of packing up and left the worrying to those whose job it was to worry—the grown-ups.

However, I don't recall why, I quickly went into the woodshed in grandmother's yard, dug up with my bare hands a very shallow dugout, and deposited into it, wrapped in cloth, mother's silver candlesticks, father's silver *talis-atara* (ornament), his Doxa pocket watch, and his silver kiddush cup that he had received as a wedding gift from either the Atzei Chaim himself or from his brother, the Satmarer Rebbe. Father's kiddush cup was used for all religious ceremonies (weddings, *brissen*, Bar Mitzvahs, etc., in our entire family). Obviously, I had the premonition that we would be away somewhere where these things wouldn't be needed or that they would be taken away from us. After the war, I retrieved those items, but, alas, some of them not for long.

The Trip to Auschwitz-Birkenau

Soon the Gestapo, the SS, and the border guards began marching us out through the gates of the Ghetto, in well-disciplined and organized groups, after warning us not to leave the formations for any reason on the pain of being shot. Somehow, it began to sink into my head that something really bad was going to happen to us. With our bundles and suitcases, we were marched through the city, which was lined with armed soldiers and policemen with submachine guns at the ready. We finally arrived at the brickyard near the main railroad station. There, the Gestapo lined us up in front of the waiting boxcar train with open doors. The Gestapo and the SS men demanded that we empty out our pockets of all valuables, diamond rings, watches, all kinds of jewelry, and especially all the money, and place them in front of us to be collected by them. We were again warned several times that if the personal searches, which were to follow soon, catch anyone holding back any valuables, he or she will be shot. More and more of us began tearing up the linings of our clothes where diamonds, gold coins, and dollar bills were sewn into them for safekeeping, and we threw them out on the piles in front of us.

Then the personal searches began. Everyone was going to be frisked. Suddenly we saw a man, Mr. Winkler, being led away in front of us, made to face us, and was shot dead, point blank, on the spot right in front of everyone because he was found to be hiding some valuables on his person. The screams of his family and of everyone else convinced us that the very last chance to get rid of all the valuables that we hoped to be able to conceal had arrived. No one needed any more persuading. As the Gestapo men walked back and forth in front of us, looking at each person they thought might still be hiding something, we were trembling with fear of being falsely accused of holding something back. This was when all of us finally realized that we were in real danger of losing our lives and that we were not merely being evacuated into the interior countryside of Hungary. The SS and Gestapo men began confiscating some of the baggage and bundles too. Grandmother, at age eighty-five or so, packed the only prized possessions she had, her *tachrichim* (shrouds) and a small pouch with "Eretz Yisroel earth" (dirt from the Holy Land), which was traditionally put into the graves of those who were buried outside Eretz Yisroel. She cried out in deep agony when an arrogant young SS guard snatched the small packet out of her hands and threw it on a garbage pile. They took away the *talis* and *tefilin* from Reb Chezkiah Greenwald who was standing near me and cried in anguish as the murderers drop-kicked it.

Finally, after standing on our feet for the better part of the day, hungry, thirsty, and terrorized, we were loaded into the wagons. We were counted, so many to each car. Some families were split up. It was very crowded. The only little windows, high up near the wagon's ceilings, were strung up with barbed wire. No food or drink was given for the journey. We had just enough space to sit on the floor with our knees at our chins. After a final demand for any valuables, the doors were shut and locked from the outside. Crying and lamenting were intermingled with heated arguments and assigning blame. Who was to be blamed for this? Where were the Judenrat people? We didn't know that they were kept back in town to assure an orderly "transfer" of the third and final transport out of the last section of the three Ghettos in town. The train finally began to move out and to pick up speed. After a while speculation began as to where we were being taken. Guesses and opinions were expressed by almost everyone. Some still believed that we were headed west into Hungary. Others, who now remembered the stories of what had happened to the deportees of 1941, were certain that we were heading eastward into Poland.

From time to time, we were halted at a siding in some town, and we were given water by the Hungarian border police, who were our armed escorts. They would not tell anyone where we were or where we were headed. Soon, someone observed through the wired windows, at a stop, that the Hungarian escort was being replaced with German Waffen-SS troops. Others were certain that they heard Polish being spoken by the railroad workers at the siding. I think that at this time everyone realized we were headed into Poland. No one fooled themselves anymore that all was going to be all right. Once in a while we stood up on our feet to let the blood circulate. Now everyone was silent and deep in their own innermost thoughts. There was no way to escape. And there was no way to imagine what we were to find at the end of the journey. We were together, the entire family next to each other. Our parents, silently, hugged and kissed us ever so often. I still had no idea of what this was all about. Nothing in my fifteen years of studying and growing up had equipped me with the tools to cope with or to rationally analyze the situation we were in. Perhaps the hunger and thirst, the exhaustion and the terror, caused me to withdraw into my shell, unable to deal with the bitter realities confronting me. I refused to think. I became totally introverted and silent. I didn't cry and I couldn't focus in on any thoughts. I was completely "out of it." I couldn't and I didn't care about anything... I was oblivious to my situation.

On Shabbat afternoon, Erev Shavuot 1944, the train arrived at its final destination. We still had no idea where we were. Both sides of the wagons' doors were flung open. Armed SS men and some guys in "striped pajamas" were screaming and beating up on us with walking canes and rifle butts, to hurry us out of the train and run in the direction of a large gate. Total chaos and confusion prevailed all around us. Anyone who carried a bundle or a suitcase was hit on the hand to drop it. Most people didn't even have the opportunity to collect their things from the wagons before they were physically pushed out. Father turned around to see where the rest of the family was. He yelled out the names of Yolika, mother, and Leitchu. I was holding on to his hand for dear life. A Gestapo trooper hooked father's head with the crooked end of a walking cane and pulled him away from the wagons by his neck like a dog, still trying to look back and screaming the names of his loved ones... I was in a complete "fog," a daze... frozen with panic and in deep shock... I had no feelings or thoughts going through my mind. I was totally passive. I just followed father, grabbing his hand ever tighter and tighter as fear and terror overtook me.

We were prodded down the long walkway to the gate, like a stampeding herd of cattle, being kicked and hit. They made sure that we didn't have the chance to look behind or around us. I was told later that we went through a gate where Gestapo officers stood with riding crops in hand and directed the oncoming herd of humans, to the right and to the left... I presume now that this was the infamous Dr. Mengele and his cohorts doing their initial "selection" of who goes to work and who goes to the gas chambers. I honestly can't remember seeing him or anyone else doing anything, except the screaming and the beatings... We were only one of many transports arriving that same day. This was where we separated from the rest of our family. Just father and I wound up together.

We still had no idea where we were or why we were there. I recall standing in formation, in a very long line, still holding onto father, on a huge parade ground. Some guys came around to cut all the hair off our heads and bodies. We remained standing there completely naked for several hours while German officers with vicious looking and growling dogs looked us over. There were no signs of the women or the children. We never saw Yolika again... I can only try to conjure up in my darkest hours of deep depression the scene of Yolika being gassed to death, screaming to father for help, with his last gasps of breath, feeling abandoned and panic stricken...

He certainly deserved to grow older. At least old enough to realize that he was NOT abandoned or ever forgotten, by his parents and siblings, who loved him so much! We never even had the chance of a final hug and of a final farewell kiss. Who knows what contributions to mankind he may have made, had he been given the chance to live... Who knows what his children would have been like... We shall never know. It is sheer torture to speculate along these lines. And it doesn't get easier or less painful with time. If at least there was a grave to go to and cry over his lost youth... What a pity that we will go down into our graves never knowing the answers to these tormenting questions. His memory lives on. Our second oldest and most wonderful grandson proudly carries his name, Yoel Elimelech Rosenfeld.

Finally, we were marched, naked, leaving our "civilian" clothes in piles in front of us on the parade grounds where we had been standing. We went to a large building, given a small bar of brownish soap (and a towel?), and herded inside in groups of perhaps two or three hundred at a time. We soaped up as soon as the water came out of the shower heads in the ceiling (honestly, no one knew at that time that in some cases deadly gas would be pumped in instead of water. I am not sure even today if the same shower barracks were used for these dual purposes). When we emerged from the showers, the first of many yet to come, we were marched out from the opposite side of the large enclosure. We were literally painted with a brush dipped in something smelling terrible, all over our bodies, to disinfect us. This procedure was repeated many times during the first few days after our arrival.

Now we were given "striped pajamas" to wear, similar to those worn by the "welcoming committee" when we arrived, and

91

some socks made out of *talis* cloth, and some shoes made of thin cloth over wooden or leather platforms. Except we didn't have the special white arm bands (or were they yellow?) that those guys had. It was getting late, almost evening. We were marched again in formation, to another parade ground. On the way, we passed close to a high, wire fence. We caught a fleeting glimpse of a group of women clinging to the other side of the fence. I heard my mother's voice calling our names. We couldn't break formation. I looked at her. Her head was as bald as ours. She had on a green evening gown, with shoulder straps. Leitchu was standing next to her, head shaved, and dressed in a flimsy dress. Mother shouted in horror: "Where is Yolika?!"... We had no answers... This was the last time we saw mother or Leitchu till after the war was over.

It got dark by the time we arrived at that other parade ground. All the time we were escorted and guarded by mean-looking SS troopers and their killer dogs. We now saw flames of a huge bonfire and columns of black smoke rising skyward in one direction of the camp. The flames lit up the sky. We also smelled the stench of burning flesh, very much like a barbecue... We still had no idea of what it was or of where in the world we were. I remember saying to father something along the lines of: "We are now at Mount Sinai about the receive the Torah! Remember, it says that they washed themselves and they changed their garments and they were told to stay away from the women... And the mountain was engulfed in fire...?!" He just squeezed my hand harder and cried.

We were taken into a nearby huge barrack building. It was a wooden structure, with two rows of triple-decked "shelves," like those you see in huge mattress warehouses. The center of the barrack was divided by a very low, but wide divider. We were ordered to climb up into those shelves and face toward the low divider in the center. There were about ten of us in each section of those large shelves. I think that there were some blankets there.

Now for the first time we were told where we were and why. A fellow inmate, in a striped uniform, with an arm band and a whip in his hand, introduced himself to us, in perfect Yiddish, as our "Block Eltester" (the man in charge of our barrack), and with him were several other guys, also with arm bands. They were introduced as our "Kappos" (barracks and camp police, they were inmates too, but obviously with a lot of power and authority over us). He began a long harangue about how happy he was to finally see us Hungarian Jews, who were so smug until now, while they were suffering in the "concentration camps" (finally we knew this was where we were) for many years. He told us with real sadistic joy that we would never leave here alive. He told us that at this very moment, our parents, our wives, and children were being gassed and burned in the camp's crematoriums. The bonfires that we saw on the way here were to take up the slack that the crematoriums could not handle when large transports were arriving.

The name of the Auschwitz–Birkenau *ka-zet* (short for concentration camp) was mentioned for the first time. We were actually in the *Cigainer lager* (Gypsy section) of the huge Birkenau *fernichtungslager* (annihilation camp) of the large and sprawling Auschwitz complex-network of camps. (Some of those were *arbeits lagers*—labor camps—while others, namely Birkenau, was the extermination camp of the entire complex.) We were given the rules of the camp. If you step outside the barracks after dark, you would be shot to death by the machine guns mounted on the guard towers, all around each compound. The women were kept in the *frauen lager* (the women's compound). Each separate compound at Birkenau was surrounded by high wire fences, while the entire outside perimeter was surrounded by additional machine gun towers and electrified wire fences. The Birkenau camp also contained the extermination compound (the gas chambers and the crematoriums section), among others.

There was the "Canada" compound, where all the materials, goods, clothing, shoes, false teeth, eyeglasses, suitcases, etc., were separated and piled up into mountains. So was the human hair shaved off all of the arrivals. There was the guards' compound and the administration or processing compound. Basically Birkenau was a processing and extermination camp. The ones who were found to be able to work would be processed in a week or two and shipped out to labor camps to do hard labor until they were no longer fit to work, then they would be returned to the extermination compound. Those who were not considered to be fit for any work, being either too young, or too old, crippled, retarded, etc., would immediately be sent to be exterminated. Very few were selected to remain in Birkenau, to assist with the processing tasks, such as our "welcoming" Kappos and other assistants, such as the "sunder commando" who actually worked the ovens, and in the Canada compound, to sort out the different "treasures" that the new arrivals brought, some of them still containing hidden valuables sewn into the clothes. We were marched around from one compound to the other, showered and disinfected almost daily; the Germans had a paranoia about outbreaks of cholera, typhus, or other infectious diseases. I have a feeling that the marches, the frequent showers, and the long hours of standing at attention on the parade grounds were meant to break our spirits into total submission and to help the SS determine who had the physical stamina to be sent to a labor camp. Every morning we were given what seemed to be a quarter of a brick-like loaf of bread, more sawdust than flour in it, some hot black drink which, for some reason, they called "coffee." At noontime we were sometimes given a very thin soup that had some green stuff floating in it. In the evening, we once again were given some of that black liquid. Not much nourishment for a still growing and very fragile teenager, or any human being, for that matter.

On the third or fourth day in Birkenau, we were marched, single file, into one of the long wooden barracks in the administration compound. We were lined up in front of some long tables, with SS men sitting behind them. We were asked our personal data—name, parents' names, birthdates, birthplaces, citizenship. The card file with this information was passed on to the next table, where some guys with fountain pens or stylus-like objects, full of ink or India ink, tattooed a number into our left forearms. It hurt very much and it was done very quickly. The ink penetrated deep under the skin. The next few days, the arms, at least mine, were swollen and infected and very painful. Once again, father went first and I followed him closely. His tattooed number was A-8530 and mine was A-8531. From that moment on we were told never again to use our names for any reason. We will appear on various work detail assignment lists and respond to roll call by that number only. In the barracks we were given narrow strips of white cloth with those numbers printed on them, followed by a yellow triangle that would identify us as Jews. There were other inmates, non-Jews, whose triangles identified them and revealed the reasons why they were there. If I remember correctly, red was for political prisoners, black was for murderers, and so on. We had to sew those strips onto the front of our jackets.

We no longer existed or mattered as human beings. We were reduced to numbers only. We certainly had no more illusions left as to who we were or as to what awaits us in the future. We were now officially *heftlinge* (inmates) or among ourselves, "Ka-Zetnicks." We had no identities left as individual beings, only as branded animals on a range, waiting to be taken to the slaughterhouse... More precisely, we were "non-humans"... We had become replaceable, exchangeable, humanoids, engraved with serial numbers, as parts of the hellish German war machine, to be discarded and disposed of, as soon as we wore out. There was no need to try to preserve us. We were available in an inexhaustible supply. As the days went on we became ever more aware of what was going on and how best to try to stay alive for another day. We learned quickly, for instance, never to volunteer for anything. One day, as we stood for hours on the *appelplatz* (roll call), a German officer announced that they need several dozen fine watchmakers and jewelers for some delicate instruments factory. Quite a few volunteers stepped forward, hoping to land some soft assignments. Within days, we found out that they were all shipped off to the coal mines... Just some morbid German humor. As a further step in the "initiation rites" into the *heftlinge* fraternity, we were taken one day as a work detail to help sort the various goods piled up, helter-skelter in large heaps, in the Canada compound. Our job was to find the various items, clean them with rags, and put each item in a separate pile. Each pile contained identical items. One had eye glasses, the other had combs, another had false teeth, one had sunglasses, another had toothbrushes, etc. Just getting to the Canada compound was probably the main objective of that exercise. We were deliberately marched by the extermination compound fence. What we saw was a scene from hell... there was a huge pile, maybe the size of a small hill, piled up with naked, dead bodies waiting to be put into the crematoriums. They were men, women, and children in one heap... Many of us began to sob silently. Others just turned the other way. I recall a terrible sickening feeling taking over my whole being. If I had any food in me, I probably couldn't have controlled myself from vomiting. My legs turned to jelly. This was our "graduation exercise." From now on we knew all that we needed to know. The picture was complete. No more illusions. No more indoctrination speeches were necessary. Any false hopes that might still have lingered on in the dark recesses of the mind were purged once and for all. This was it. Here is where we will all end up, sooner or later. The rest of our days would be devoted to the task of postponing that inevitable day to "later" rather than "sooner." The years of intensive therapy have not succeeded to completely erase the horror of that mountain of human bodies from my memory.

For many years I was tormented in my sleep with nightmarish glimpses of those corpses. However, as the years go on, over 60 years now, the nightmares that used to torment all of my nights are less frequent.

The daily showers and disinfections continued. After several days, perhaps a week or ten days after we arrived, we were told that we were being marched off to a labor camp. From old-time inmates we had learned to appreciate this as the best news possible. The farther you got away from Birkenau, the better the odds were for survival, especially if you were lucky enough not to wind up in a coal mine. Chances were good that in a "productive" camp, at least as long as your health and strength held out, you would escape the dreaded *selekcias* (the selections of the infirm and the non-productive *heftlinge*, to return to Birkenau for disposal). The labor camps offered some routines and a small measure of stability. You were more likely to receive your daily food rations regularly in a labor camp rather than in the extermination camp of Birkenau.

Of course, we had no idea where we were to be taken.

BUNA-MONOWITZ

One morning, after we were given our bread portion for the day, counted out, and our serial numbers registered on a clipboard, a platoon or so of the Waffen-SS were attached to us and we began our march out from the Hell on Earth that was Birkenau. The guards placed themselves at strategic intervals, with their machine pistols at the ready, pointed at us all the time. We actually passed through the gates of Birkenau, perhaps through the same gates that we passed through on the way in, what seemed now to have been ages ago... We were marching in military formations, counting cadence. But not singing... We marched on the main roads competing with civilian and military transport of all descriptions. We marched through populated villages and towns, in our distinct striped pajamas. So much for the claim of the civilians after the war that they had no idea that there were concentration camps within their districts. Everyone saw us and knew who we were.

We marched, at least several thousands of us—most of us were survivors from our original transport from Chust—for about ten or twelve miles, non-stop. Finally we arrived, in late afternoon, to a "beautiful" camp with two-story brick buildings. Here I saw for the first time the wrought-iron arch over the gate with the motto "*Arbeit Macht Frei*" (Work Liberates) in huge latticework letters on it. I was still holding on tight to father's hand for dear life. This we were told was "Auschwitz Camp." It looked unbelievably different from the camp we left behind. Here, the *heftlinge* wore better clothing than we did. They had regular shoes on. Some of them even wore civilian clothes with a swatch of the striped blue and white (pajama) material replacing a cut hole in the back of the jackets and a red stripe down the trousers. The "barracks" were real houses, with rooms divided, on each of the two floors of each cottage. There were flower beds with pretty flowers all around each cottage. The food (supper) was much thicker than the watery "soup" we got used to in Birkenau.

Panic struck me when the Kappo or other "functionary" counted out the number of inmates to be placed in each cottage overnight and ended his count right between father and me! I was certain that I would never see him again. He tried to reassure me, in a whisper, that he would see me in the morning. I was not so sure. The beds here were "comfortable" in comparison to the "stalls" of Birkenau. They were relatively soft, with some sort of army issue mattresses and covered with a blanket. Father was right. In the morning we saw each other again. He was billeted in the cottage next to where I was. We were fed again, bread and "coffee," and marched off to the showers to be disinfected again. As usual, we left all our clothes in the anteroom and walked in naked into the shower room and came out after the showers at the opposite end, where we received "new" clothes. There was never the slightest chance of keeping anything, personal mementos of any kind, between "before and after" the showers. After the showers, the whole group was reassembled at an *appelplatz*. I found father and we were "reattached" once again. We were now on our way to another, unknown destination. After the war, I became aware of the fact that this was the "model" or "show" camp of the whole Auschwitz complex of camps. Here the Red Cross inspectors as well as other foreign visitors were taken to be convinced that we were treated "humanely." Those *heftlinge* that were stationed here permanently, those who made up the infrastructure and assisted in the administration of this particular camp, were indeed the lucky few. They had it much easier than the rest of the inmates of other concentration camps.

We marched, once again, on the main roads and encountered civilians and regular army troops, as we marched in formation.

Finally, after about ten or twelve miles, we arrived at another camp that looked much more like the one in Birkenau. Except it had no gas chambers or crematoriums. Here, once again, were the familiar long wooden barracks. The perimeters were guarded the same way as in Birkenau: double fences, one was electrified with high voltage, and watchtowers with machine-gun nests were all over the place.

There were three internally fenced-off areas, not electrified and without guard towers. One separated the inmates' barracks from the administration, the guards' quarters, kitchen and supply buildings. The second fence, separated everyone from the "entertainment" barracks, where some women were kept locked up all the time. We could hear them but never saw them. The third fence separated the "Krankenbau" (infirmary) from the rest of the camp. It was a large and sprawling camp. There were also two huge, temporary tents, "Zelt 1" and "Zelt 2," set up in the middle of the camp, on part of the *appelplatz*, to accommodate the extra influx of *heftlinge* that were coming in daily from Hungary and later on from the Lodz Ghetto, the last one left in Poland.

We quickly found out that this was to be our permanent labor camp. It was called "Buna" because of the huge "Bunawerk" factory nearby, where we and prisoners of war from England, Canada, and Russia were employed as forced laborers. The little village nearby, in Upper Selesia, was called Monovitze in Polish and Monowitz in German. This camp, too, was part of the enormous Auschwitz complex of camps. As my luck would have it, I was once again separated from father by the count ending just between us. This time it was permanent. I got into one of the regular barracks, #53, I think, and father wound up in "Zelt 2." It turned out to be a good thing. We were assigned to two different work "Commandos" (details). I did not have to see him suffer during the day at hard labor and he did not see me. I was assigned to "Commando 200." I don't remember father's assignment.

Each commando was assigned a Kappo who acted as the responsible "foreman" of the commando. Some commandos had many hundreds of *heftlinge* in them. In those cases there were one head Kappo and many sub-Kappos as assistants. These were privileged positions. They wielded great power over the inmates. Most of them were hardened inmates who survived by cunning and sheer instinct. Some of them were German criminals, murderers, and other misfits. They had better clothes, better food, and they could move around freely in the huge factory and made contact with some of the prisoners of war and Polish civilian workers, and received extra food from them.

Every morning, we were out of the barracks before dawn, to stand in formation, each barrack separately, with the *blokelterster* (the head of each barrack) counting the prisoners and reporting the numbers to the *lagerelterster* (the chief of the camp). These were all fellow prisoners, but with great authority and real powers over our lives. The *lagerelterster* was a German criminal or murderer. He wore civilian clothes with his number printed on a swatch of white linen over the little pocket of his jacket. He in turn reported the numbers of prisoners still alive and present and the numbers who had died during the night or who had been shipped out to other camps to the SS Commandant of the camp. This took a long time. In the cold winter days we froze in the harsh early morning frost of this part of Poland, where Auschwitz was located. Those who were really sick reported that fact to the barrack chief and were sent off under SS guards to the Krankenbau, where fellow inmates who identified themselves to the Germans as physicians tried their best to help, if they had an Aspirin or a crepe-paper bandage to cover a wound.

It was a very dangerous place to be when the German camp doctor came around and decided that you were "terminal," wrote down your number, and you would be taken, in a closed "ambulance" truck, back to Birkenau for final disposal. Some took a chance anyway. One day my fingers were oozing with puss from frostbite wounds. I couldn't feel anything in those frozen digits. I went to the infirmary. An inmate doctor cut out the infected areas with a pair of ordinary scissors, put some iodine on them and bandaged them up with some paper and whispered in my ear, in Hungarian, not to stay there, but to ask to be taken back to the barracks, because rumor had it that a "medical team" from Birkenau was on the way to all the labor camps to make *selekcias* in the infirmaries, to get rid of the "malingerers" and of the really sick people.

If a prisoner could not be accounted for, we had to stand in formation for many hours until they found him, or go back to the barracks and wait for the "Toten Kopf" (with the skull and cross bones insignia) SS guards to come into each barrack and count heads.

After the morning count, the *appel*, we were taken back to the barracks and given the daily portion of bread and coffee. Now we were reassembled on the *appelplatz* in formations by commando units. Each commando had an assigned place on the parade grounds to assemble in the morning and to march to in the evening when they returned from the factory.

Bunawerk was a huge, sprawling factory. It was surrounded by many prisoner of war camps. It was across the road from our camp. The factory was in reality an entire city, with hundreds of buildings and several tens of thousands of forced laborers. It belonged to the giant I.G. Farben Industries of Germany. I don't know to this day what exactly was manufactured there. It was so huge that no one was familiar with the total factory and its purpose. We, the *heftlinge* from camp Buna, mostly worked on construction sites. We dug deep ditches for building foundations, unloaded trainloads of cement, mixed and poured the cement into those ditches. Other commandos worked with the iron poles to reinforce the concrete. Others worked as "mechanics"

102

to prepare all the needed tools to do the job. I don't think that any of us actually worked inside one of those manufacturing buildings where production took place.

There was always a very strong, sweet odor from the steam pipes that carried the excess steam out of the buildings. Some people said that the factory was producing margarine and other edible oils from coal. Others were certain that gasoline, rubber, and soap were made from the abundant trainloads of coal that were constantly being unloaded at the factory.

The first time a sack of cement was put on my shoulders for me to carry it from the train to the storage shack, I immediately fell forward with my face to the ground, the heavy load pinning my head to the muddy ground. The Polish civilian supervisor of that building site muttered with clenched teeth in a heavy Slavic-accented German: *"Du ferfluchter jude – du bist nisht wert das brot was du est"* (You accursed Jew – you don't even deserve the bread that you eat). I was terrified that he would hand me over to the Kappo as a malingerer. Instead, he put me together with another sixteen- or seventeen-year-old boy inside the shack to stack those sacks of cement.

Every morning, after the *appel* was over, we were escorted by heavily armed Toten Kopf Waffen-SS guards into the factory and delivered us to the various work sites. The civilian contractors, some Polish and some German, took charge of us and told the Kappos what needed to be done. The Kappos saw to it that the work was done by beating and kicking us and threatening reports to the chief Kappos. The work was backbreaking. We got a half hour break for "lunch" (a water-thin soup with an occasional piece of something solid—a piece of some vegetable, perhaps—floating in it). But mercifully it was always hot and we got to sit down for that half hour to rest. We named it "Buna Soup." Sometimes we went searching around the outside of the buildings for something edible. With luck, we would occasionally

103

find a piece or two of raw potato peels. We put them on the jets of steam escaping from the pipes to "cook" and we ate the delicacy with zest.

We were marched to work while a musical band made up of inmates were playing Wagner and other classical music. When we returned to camp at the end of the hard working day once again the band greeted us at the gate. We only had to cross the main road, in and out of camp to the factory. The SS troops blocked the road, some on motorcycles, while we marched by. It took a very long time for the entire work force to pass by. The military prisoners of war were housed in different camps surrounding the factory. Some *heftlinge* had the good fortune of actually seeing and talking at work with some Canadian prisoners, and they even received some food from them, even a piece of chocolate, from the Red Cross packages that they received. I was never that lucky.

Upon the return from work we were again lined up by commando formations on the *appelplatz* to be counted again and reports made up the chain of command. Only then, after an hour or so, were we dismissed to our barracks. We lined up in front of the barracks and were called by serial numbers to receive "dinner," a piece of the so-called bread and a cup of that "coffee." Most of the rest of the time we were now free to do what needed to be done—wash ourselves by the long line of faucets with cold water or rinse out our clothes. We had access to needle and yarn from the barracks functionaries to mend torn garments. We could line up in front of the barracks' barber to have our heads and/or beards shaved. The Germans were strict about hair. They were petrified of lice-born diseases spreading epidemics not just among the inmates but also among the military personnel and the surrounding civilian villagers.

This was the time when my father and I got together to do those chores and to wonder about the rest of the family. "Where is mother now? I wonder if Leitchu is with mother. Who knows what happened to Yolika?" These were the daily openers that led to nostalgic memories of the good old days. Quite often father would give me an extra piece of bread, which he said he got from a Polish foreman at work. I know for a fact that some of that bread was also paid for with some of his gold crowns that he tore off his own teeth. He constantly looked out for me as much as was humanly possible under the circumstances. We talked a great deal every day before going off to our separate sleeping places.

Some days we knew immediately, after crossing the road back from work, that we "were in for it." As the music was playing, we could spot a large contingent of extra guards waiting for us just inside the gates. That usually meant either that some high "brass" was coming to look us over, or that there was going to be a *selekcia*. But most often it meant that there was going to be a public execution by hanging. We really didn't feel so much sorry for the poor, hapless victims; we were much too hardened for that kind of "luxury," as we felt terribly sorry for ourselves. It meant that we would have to stand on the *appelplatz* for additional long hours, waiting for the camp Commandant and his staff to finish their dinner and come out to the *appelplatz*, read the Courts Marshal verdict, give us a speech about the dangers of stealing food from the kitchen or of trying to escape, two of the most common "crimes" for which these victims paid with their lives. After the hanging ceremony was over, we all marched by the gallows in formation, to view the bodies while the band played on. Only then would we be counted, reported, and dismissed to the barracks to receive our dinner. It took about two or three hours of extra time standing on our feet tired and hungry... At the tender age of sixteen, I witnessed twenty-eight such executions in Buna, usually in groups of three or four at a time.

One rainy day, I was petrified when I met my father after work. He had unloaded sacks of cement all day in the rain. Some of the cement dust mixed with raindrops and hardened on the nape of his neck into a solid chunk of concrete. He couldn't move his head. Slowly and I am sure, painfully, I helped him chip away the mess, a little piece at the time, with the spoon we had for the Buna soup. We often compared our day's experiences at work. He cried about my fate and I cried about his. He had to watch helplessly as his son suffered so much pain and stress. And I had the great misfortune of watching my father, my hero, whom I had worshiped as the greatest human being alive, my teacher and mentor, suffering humiliation and torment. It was sheer agony for both of us, not just physical but mostly emotional.

If I remember correctly, and I am no longer certain that I do, we were off from work on Sundays, one week a full day and the other week, from noon on. This gave us some breathing time and more opportunities to be together with father. We would do our chores and sometimes just visit some of our other relatives, uncles and cousins who were in the same camp with us. This free time was not always a given. Sometimes the SS men would round up some of the strolling inmates and take them on special work details in the camp itself or in the factory. One Sunday father got caught in this net, without me knowing about it. I was petrified with panic that something has happened to him and that I would be left to survive on my own. I was completely convinced that I could never make it on my own without father's constant advice, encouragement to persevere, and his reassuring faith that we will soon be redeemed from this hell. The *mashiach* (redeemer) must be on his way. All the Holy Scriptures and our Sages of old had predicted this inhuman suffering just prior to the final redemption.

The free periods in camp often turned into terror by the sound of a motorcycle's roar. It meant "run for cover, the *malach hamavet* (angel of death) is on the loose." This guy was a junior grade Waffen-SS, Toten Kopf officer, in a leather jacket, with his girlfriend in the back seat, roaming through the camp with pistol in hand, shooting at will any inmate that he felt like should be "terminated" on the spot. He and his girlfriend were laughing hilariously at this sportsman's shooting gallery victims. We saw him riding his motorbike, back and forth, while we were marched to and back from work. He must have been in charge of the guards who were responsible to watch us against escape attempts. There were very few such attempts. They were doomed to fail from the start.

Almost every night, though, the silence was pierced by machine gun fire from the watchtowers and by the shrill sounds of the sirens. In the mornings we would see one or more lifeless bodies stuck on the electrified fence. These were the ones who could no longer wait for the *mashiach*. They wanted out, now! Their bodies were left there for everyone to see the futility of trying to escape. Some had no intention of escaping at all. They just wanted to commit suicide. And they succeeded.

Interestingly, most of those suicides were not "our kind" of people. They were for the most part either German Jews who always considered themselves as good, loyal Germans. Unlike those backward, filthy-looking, bearded *Ost Yuden* (Eastern Jews, like us), whom they despised as primitive beggars, they were highly educated and deeply assimilated into the cultural elite of German society. Others were the "white arm band" inmates. These were Christian Germans, or so they thought for many generations. These were churchgoers. Only when the Nazis began to check their "pedigrees" they discovered that there was at least 1/8 part of Jewish blood in their polluted arteries. They really had a very hard time understanding how they wound up with us *Ost Yuden*.

These two groups, who had put their complete trust in the civilized "Humanism" of the German culture, could not cope with the reality of the bankruptcy of that "faith." They saw no way out. There was no *mashiach* coming to free them. We, on the other hand, were certain that all of this suffering had been predicted in the Holy Scriptures, and so was the redemption. We

107

just had to persevere. Didn't Daniel say: *"Ashrei hamechake veyagia lekeitz hayumim"*? (Happy will be those who will persevere, and hope to reach the End of the Days—the coming of the *mashiach*). So we continued to hope and wait for the End of the Days to arrive while we were still around to enjoy it. We continued to pray daily and try to improve our ways, do *teshuvah* (repentance) for our sins... So we did not run to the electrified wires. The routines of camp life and the quest for survival kept us going. Every week or so, we "lost" some of our relatives and friends from home. We never knew if they were transferred to some other camp (there were dozens of them working the coal mines who constantly needed new replacements for the "worn out parts"), or if they were caught during one of the ever more frequent *selekcias* and wound up back in Birkenau.

Some of those who disappeared were my uncles Yoel and Hershel, the *dayan*, who lived across the street from us and whose children were Leitchu's and my friends, Reb Shmiel Frankel, the unofficial Rav of the Atzei Chaim Beis Medrish, Reb Shmiel Brach, and many others.

Around October 1944, some of us got together in one barrack, after work, to recite by heart as many of the Rosh Hashanah and Yom Kippur prayers that we could recall, each one contributing what he remembered. Yom Kippur eve, father was the *shaliach tzibur* at the far end of my barrack, with our "lookouts" posted. His *Kol Nidrei* that evening, in hushed, choking, and heart-rending tones must have reached the *kissei hakavod* (G-d's Holy Throne). We all cried for our loved ones and for ourselves. As long as I live I will never forget that solemn and purifying prayer. Father and I cried together, after the formal prayers, for our loved ones...

On Yom Kippur day, at work in the trenches that we were digging, each one of us fasting (no big effort was needed, we had plenty of practice), we gathered at lunchtime in one of those trenches to pray. Once again, each one contributed what they could remember. Father was not there. He worked at some other place. My contribution was the *L'(K)eil Orech Din.* I remembered every one of the alphabetical verses. We did our best... At night we broke our fast with the extra piece of "bread," which we saved from the morning. It was very hard to hide anything in the barracks. Whatever was left unguarded was stolen. Our bodies were subject to searches. When taken to the showers, everything was left behind, so it was not easy to hide the extra bread portions that we saved for breaking the fast.

Each barrack had several rows of triple-decker bunkbeds, in very neat order. Between each long row of twin beds, there were spacious aisles. The *blokelterster* had a small room to himself at the entrance to the barrack. There were about 200–250 inmates in each barrack. The two huge tents held about 500 or more inmates each. At night there were several buckets at the end of the barrack to serve as latrines, since we were not permitted to leave the barrack at night. Every morning the *blockelterster* would pick at random a few people, as they were making up their beds to serve as the "Scheiss Commando." Their job was to empty the buckets, clean and disinfect them. Not a very pleasant task. Sometimes a few people were assigned to that commando for a long period of time as punishment for some minor infractions of the rules (beds not made up properly, torn jacket, etc.). During the day, we used the camp latrines (there were a few of them scattered throughout the camp). These were long barracks with several dozen "seats," in long rows in multiple sections. From time to time, unlucky inmates were assigned to the "Latrine Scheiss Commando." Their job, which lasted for days at a time, was to clean the entire latrine ditch—a horrible assignment.

Life went on as a routine. The main and most immediate goals of life were to get an extra piece of bread, any way possible. Stealing from each other was one of the most common ways to do it (we called this activity "organizing"). Trying to avoid the Angel of Death on his motorcycle was another priority. Planning and scheming how to avoid being caught for extra work on Sundays and for "Scheiss Commando" duty took all the cunning and energy one could muster. Plans for escape never even entered our minds. There simply was no way in the world that it could succeed. Non-Jewish Polish or German inmates who knew the country and the language and had some relatives or contacts on the outside were the only ones who could ever hope to make it. They were, usually, the ones who wound up on the gallows anyway.

One Sunday afternoon around the beginning of the winter, October or November, as we were going about the camp, doing our chores, the sirens began howling. We all ran back into our barracks as we were trained to do in such cases. Suddenly we saw, heard, and felt actual bombs falling all around us in the camp and in the factory. Most of us were delighted. It was a sure sign that the front is moving closer to us and that soon we would be redeemed. I don't know if anyone was killed during that bombing raid or not. But I do remember that one or two bombs did become embedded into the *appelplatz*, without exploding, and we watched the German soldiers from afar disarming and dismantling them. From that day on, almost daily raids occurred at almost the exact same time, around noon. No big damage, if any, was done to the factory. They were more an annoyance than anything else for the Germans. However, to us, the whining of those engines of the allied bombers every day and the wailing of the sirens were a blessing. Not only did they forecast defeat for the Germans in the near future, but of more immediate benefit was the fact that while the air raid was going on, sometimes for an entire hour or so, we could take shelter in one of the many concrete-lined building foundations and rest.

Only one time do I remember a very heavy bombing raid that came too close to where we were huddling for safety. The bombs were whistling fiercely in a menacing shrill, as they were

THE PRINCIPAL

cutting through the air. It seemed for a while that the pressure over our heads alone would do us in. The bombs were exploding all around us. One exploded in the same foundation trench where we were, just at the far end of it, perhaps several dozen yards from where we were. The concussion slammed us against the concrete wall and to the ground. I was certain that the next one would actually kill us.

Around this time, my left leg became irritated and a nasty looking blister formed just below the ankle and above the heel, from the constant friction of the "shoe" as I walked. One morning, several weeks later, the blister had developed into a very ugly puss-filled boil. I continued limping to work as best I could, in spite of it. One morning as I woke up, I was no longer able to stand on that leg at all. Red streaks spread from the scab all the way up to the underside of my knee. The pain was unbearable. I began to shiver with fever. Father and I tried to put cold compresses on the infected areas, to no avail. I had no choice but to take my chances at the Krankenbau, knowing full well the danger involved in getting caught there during a *selekcia*. But by now I had reached the point where I had given up on surviving. I was by this time not much more than a limping skeleton.

We had all noticed something that made this decision easier. Lately, toward the end of November, there seemed to have come an end to the dreaded, weekly *selekcias*, where we all had to strip naked at one end of the barrack, walk across to the far end where the SS doctor would decide if our turn had come to go back to Birkenau, or if we still had enough flesh and muscle left to continue to work for a while longer. For some reason, we were not subjected to this procedure for a few weeks now. This was the reason that I was able to limp along for some time without being "selected."

After the war I heard two different versions of why this happened. One was that the Germans began to dismantle the gas chambers and the crematoriums, in order to destroy the evidence

111

of what the extermination compound was really like. The other version claimed that some of the "sonder commando" inmates, the ones who actually worked the ovens, with the help of some Polish underground fighters, had succeeded in blowing up the death factory. I never found out which version, if either, was the truth. But at the time, we began to be less afraid to go to the "hospital" (the Krankenbau) than before.

I was immediately assigned to a bunk in one of the three Krankenbau barracks. There must have been at least 200 or more patients in each of them. The staff consisted of *heftlinge* who claimed to be doctors. By now I had a large "pouch" filled with puss under my knee. The infection was now in my entire left leg all the way up to my crotch. I could not stand at all, nor could I stretch my leg out straight. The chief surgeon in this barrack was a Prof. Dr. Lengyel, who I was told after the war was in charge of his own surgical clinic in Klausenburg (Cluj), a Hungarian-occupied big city in Rumania. He decided to operate on me, to open up the pouch and let the puss drain out. Of course there was no anesthetic or any other kinds of medication. He literally knocked me out with a huge fist to my jaw. It worked... I was out cold. When I came to, I was hurting terribly. The crepe-paper bandage was oozing with blood and puss. I was still burning with fever. The infection was to stay with me for months to come.

The scar tissue was forming around the incision. But since I couldn't stretch out my leg at all, the tissue and skin grew and fused a part of my leg to my thigh. After a few weeks my knee seemed to have become the end of my leg. I could not eat anything. Just sipped some liquids. Dr. Lengyel tried valiantly to feed me some bread and to change the paper bandages as often as he could. I was rapidly deteriorating. Father came every day after work to stay with me, try to feed me, and to encourage me to hold on a little longer; soon we would be freed.

I remained in that Krankenbau getting thinner and weaker every day. The fever never let up. The bombings continuously went on outside. We could even hear what seemed to be artillery explosions from far away. On January 18th (I was later told), my father came to see me for the very last time. He cried bitterly that he had to leave me behind, since all who were still able to walk were being withdrawn westward. We said our goodbyes knowing full well that we would never see each other again... Father begged me to forgive him for all the bad things he had done to me. He asked forgiveness for bringing me to this place rather than to have tried to save us when he could... He cried and hugged and kissed me apologizing for abandoning me. I cried with all energy that was left in me. I knew, and father knew, that it was just a matter of a few days before I would die from the terrible infection and hunger... So this was it, the final separation... never to see each other again...

THE RUSSIANS ARE COMING—RETREAT

On that day, Thursday, January 18, 1945, all of the inmates, tens of thousands, were marched out of Camp "Buna" in different directions, fleeing before the attacking Russian army from the east. The only ones remaining in camp were us, in the Krankenbau and, we later found out, that several dozen of "able-bodied" *heftlinge*, mostly old-time veterans with many years of experience in survival techniques, also hid underneath some barracks, to await the arrival of the Russians.

That Thursday night the almost empty and ghostly camp, especially the Krankenbau, with its remaining live skeletons, was subjected to merciless fire-bombing and machine-gun strafings from the air. We didn't know then, and I still don't know today, if it was the Russians "softening up" what must have seemed to them from the air as huge army barracks, or if it was the Germans, attempting to obliterate all traces of what they left behind. To us it really didn't matter very much who was going to kill us. My barrack too was in flames. I was immobile, still burning with high fever. No able-bodied people at all were left in the Krankenbau to look after us. The windows were shattered from the explosions. The frost of the January night was mercilessly biting our remaining bits of flesh. The flames were now engulfing all the surrounding barracks too. Utter despair and panic took over. To my luck, Hashem provided me with a Guardian Angel, in the person of Dr. Korach. He was a pharmacist in Chust. He and his other brother, Dr. Korach, the ophthalmologist, came to settle in Chust with their families when the Hungarians took over. They were "Neolog" or Reform Jews. This Dr. Korach, the pharmacist, was lying in the bed next to mine. I don't recall when he came there. He was able to move about much better than I could. I don't recall why he was there. He grabbed me by one arm, wrapped me in several blankets, and dragged me from my lower bunk, on to the floor and out into the snow. I was shivering with fever and terror. We watched part of the long barrack being charred badly before the fire subsided. He then dragged me back into my bunk, covered me with some extra blankets that were abandoned by some inmates who didn't make it back in but froze to death during the night on the snow. He kept forcing some bits of snow into my mouth to save me from total dehydration.

These bids of snow that he forced into my mouth and the lying in the snow for a long time that night probably helped break the fever. He kept on "lecturing" me not to give up now when we are so close to become free people again; it would be a great sin to give up and die now! He took some crumbs of bread that he had stashed away, rolled them in some snow and force-fed me. He just wouldn't give up on me. He also decided that it wouldn't be worth staying alive, if I would remain crippled with my leg. So he began, a little at a time, to pull my leg away from my thigh, tearing the scar tissue a bit at a time every few hours, every day, until I was finally able to almost completely stretch out my leg. The puss and the blood kept on oozing from the wide-open gap underneath my knee. Now he said it was time to begin learning how to stand up again, and later on learn how to walk again. I held onto the middle bunks in the aisles trying to stand on the "good," right leg. I promptly collapsed. My leg had no muscles left on it to support even the twenty-seven kilograms (about sixty lbs.) of my total weight! I was truly just a skeleton covered with loosely hanging skin. This existence in no-man's land lasted for ten days, while the bombing and artillery fire shook the ground beneath us.

About four or five days after the camp was abandoned by the retreating Germans, a few truckloads of Waffen-SS men came to camp and asked by megaphones for all able-bodied people to assemble to receive bread rations. A few of the more trusting, desperate souls, about fifteen or so of those who were smart enough to hide out at the time of the evacuation just a few days earlier, actually assembled around the trucks, where upon the Germans promptly executed them on the spot and left. For some unexplained reason, they never came to the Krankenbau.

During the ten days after the evacuation, we received no food or water at all; we were just left to die out in no-man's land. There was no need to waste food or bullets on us. Nature would take care of us. And indeed nature did! From the over 200 patients in my barrack alone, only about 50 or so lasted long enough to see the liberators enter the camp. Those of us who were still alive just waited for them to die so that we could quickly grab their blankets and any food they may have left behind their pillows. Often while pulling on the blankets, the corpses would come tumbling down to the floor, too. They remained there rotting away. The live ones relieved themselves on the floor from their perches in the bunks. No one wanted or could get out of bed for such a "trivial" function. The floors in the barracks were covered with thick frozen layers of excrement and urine mingled with the dead bodies...

For ten days we remained stuck in the limbo of no-man's land between the German and Russian armies. We could hear the constant, by now familiar thumps of exploding shells. At times, they seemed to be quite close and at other times far away. Apparently the front changed hands several times during those ten days. The Germans just would not give up the giant "Buna" factory without a major battle. On January 27th during the morning hours of "Shabbat Shira" (Shabbat of Song), the first Russian tanks and infantry entered camp "Buna." The Russians were totally bewildered and confused by what they saw. At first they were sure that we were German criminals or deserters.

We were the very first concentration camp on the path of this particular Division. Some of us tried our broken and halting Ukrainian dialects on them to try to explain to them that we were Jewish forced-labor inmates who were too sick to be withdrawn and that we hadn't eaten in ten days. As combat units, they did the best that they could before pressing on forward. They provided us with some of the same food they ate. They shot a horse, cooked it with beans and cabbage and fed us. This kind of heavy food, of course, was absolute poison for us. From among those who survived till now, more than half died that night from overeating that heavy food. Only about twenty of us remained alive the next morning. Dr. Korach would not allow me to touch that food at all. He kept on feeding me ever larger crumbs of bread moistened with snow.

The next morning, some support units of the Russian army arrived, with the occupying forces, after the forward, combat units left. A matronly army physician with some nurses came to look at us. It turned out that she spoke fluent Yiddish. We explained to her exactly who we were. She cried bitterly. She had seen Birkenau on her way to us. She first gave us all Aspirins and some vitamin C tablets. She then ordered to round up some Polish civilians from the nearby town of Monowitze, to bury the dead and to clean up the floors with pickaxes and shovels. Others were ordered to board up the broken windows and to put in wood burning stoves in the barracks and keep the fires going all day and night long. Some of those civilians were crying and crossing themselves at the horrible sight. Others were cursing us and the soldiers for making them do the filthy work. They too protested that they had no knowledge of what was happening in the camps. Now that we had a stove in the barrack, Dr. Korach made me some toast on top of the stove and melted some snow for drinking water. I was beginning to be able to stretch my leg more and more often and with less excruciating pain than before.

The wound under my knee remained open with puss coming out of it. The Russians began to bandage up that wound as best they could under field conditions.

On the third or fourth day after the liberation, the Russian army brought in more nurses and permanently assigned them to us; they began to bathe us, disinfect us, and look after our wounds. We were weighed (twenty-seven kg.) and given clean, striped pajamas. The next day, a Red Cross worker (or perhaps it was a social worker) came in to interview us for the most essential, personal data such as name, age, hometown, citizenship, serial number, etc.

We were now transferred back by military ambulances to the main Auschwitz camp, the one we passed on the way to Buna, with the brick cottages and the flower gardens. We were housed in the hospital of the camp, which was clean and warm. Army and civilian doctors took care of us now. We were still trying to "organize" and eat as much food as we could put our hands on. One of the few able-bodied inmates who remained hidden in the main camp was a young man from Teich who had studied with me at the yeshivah in Chust. The day after we came to the hospital, I heard a voice calling out in Yiddish, asking if there was anyone here from Teich or from Chust. I was lying flat on my back at the time. I called out to him that I was from both Teich and Chust. I had no idea at first who he was until he approached my bunk. We immediately recognized each other and began to hug and cry. He looked quite healthy. Apparently he was among the luckier ones who spent most of his time at that main show camp and had access to plenty of extra food.

It seems that the retreating SS handed over to some of the remaining inmates who dared to come out from hiding after the general retreat the keys to the well-stocked food and clothing warehouses in the camp. He asked me if I was hungry and what I would like to eat. Soon he came back with a whole wooden case of smelly "quargel" cheese and a few large cans of cooked beef. This time Dr. Korach allowed me to eat some of the cheese with some real bread and even a few pieces of the meat. The rest we shared with the other recuperating former inmates.

The doctors and nurses continued treating our wounds. They worked with me daily to exercise my left leg and to get me to be able to use my right leg as best as they could. After a few weeks, the ones who were able to leave began to find their way back home. At this time Dr. Korach too said his goodbyes to me and left. I was never able to find out what had happened to this noble angel of mercy. I hope that he made it to wherever he was going and that he was able to find some survivors of his family to begin life anew. He certainly deserved it.

My leg would not heal. After several weeks at the main camp hospital, those of us who still needed active medical intervention were transferred to the civilian hospital in the town of Oswiencin (Auschwitz). Here the International Red Cross continued to provide the assistance to the patients. About the end of February or so, I was able to hop along on my right leg with the support of two crutches. I was allowed to go into town with some other recuperating inmates. We were still wearing our prison outfits, except that these were no longer the "striped pajama" types. These were the former civilian suits or sports jackets, with a window cut into the back, patched up with striped material to identify us as former *heftlinge*. We did have some civilian shirts that we "organized" (stole) from the camp supply warehouses. Oswiencin was a small town with some stores and shops. As we passed a delicatessen, my eyes caught a plate of schmaltz herring roe in the window. I had dreamed in my time of hunger that I was eating a full plate of herring roe with a whole loaf of fresh bread with butter, chased down with a liter or so of fresh cold milk... I could not contain myself. I walked in the store and with my broken Czech and German persuaded the storekeeper to trade

119

me a plate of the roe with bread and butter for two shirts (one off my back). It was the first time I really enjoyed myself in a very long time... It was a dream come true.

HOPE AND REALITY

After father was evacuated from Buna, together with the rest of the inmates, we never heard from them or about them. I was hoping against all odds that father also survived, and that he was heading home to meet up with the rest of the family. Only much later did I find out that hope has very little in common with reality.

The reality was heartbreaking. The evacuees were force-marched to various camps all over Austria and Germany. Some were force-marched for many days without any food or water. Others were packed into cattle cars and shuffled around between cities for many days at a time. Those who fell out of formation were summarily executed on the spot.

While I was already dreaming and fantasizing of a reunited family as a free human being, they—father, mother, and Leitchu—were still suffering, worse than ever before. Yolika, of course, no longer suffered. He was free from suffering from day one of our arrival in Birkenau.

After a long and torturous march, father finally arrived in the notorious Buchenwald concentration camp, somewhere in Germany. One of my surviving cousins told me after the war of meeting him there. With great sorrow father had told him that I was no longer alive... He was convinced that the infection, the fever, and the starvation had killed me. The greatest tragedy of all was the fact that he survived all the suffering and torture, both physical and emotional, until about eight days before the liberation of his camp. He came so close and paid such a hefty price trying to survive, but he never made it. What a pity!

Now that I was sure to survive, physically at least, my emotional and spiritual torment began. Until now, all my energies and thoughts were concentrated only on the primary, basic needs: how to get some more food and how to stay alive. Now suddenly, I became aware that I could think and feel again. I realized now that I was sixteen years old, a teenager, without a home, without parents, and without a future. How would I ever find out what happened to my family? How would I find them? How would I let them know that I was alive?!

As if this was not tormenting enough, I was "punished" with an inquiring mind. I began searching deep in my soul and my mind, to try to understand what had just happened to us as a family, as a community, as a nation, and as the "chosen people" of G-d. Chosen for what? What about all of those great scholars and pious elders of our town whom I had seen killed or tortured? Were they less observant and less deserving of life than me? Was my saintly old grandmother less deserving of a peaceful death than I was? What about the promised *mashiach*—where was he? What was he waiting for? If not now, when? These questions were heresy till now. A good *yeshivah bochur*, and a Satmar Hasid, just doesn't allow himself to ask such questions. I would surely be punished for allowing my mind to question G-d's judgments. But how could I control these sad thoughts?! I was frightened, tormented, and disturbed by these totally unfamiliar questions and thoughts. They made me angry at myself and at the whole mass that forced me into these lines of thinking. I was torn apart inside. I cried at night and was tormented during the day. What am I going to do? How will I ever find guidance to help me sort out those terrible questions and find answers that will bring me solace and some semblance of peace of mind? Deep feelings of guilt, without realizing it, for remaining alive, and for not making an attempt to persuade father to stay with me in Buna drove me close to complete insanity. Would he have stayed, risking both of our lives? Maybe, but I will never know for sure. This is a very heavy burden on me. I had become aware, very quickly and at an age too young to cope, that "freedom" is only a relative concept. I was free in body but not in spirit. I was very confused and troubled. My real Holocaust awareness had just begun. My self-assurance as a human being and my confidence in myself and in what I had been taught, which I should have developed during those teenage years, never had a chance to fully develop. I still suffer from those feelings of guilt even as a fully-grown adult. My self-image remains that of a tormented lost soul, suffering from those terrible events of my youth. I was still hopping along on my two crutches. My wound refused to heal. In the civilian hospital in the town of Auschwitz, under the Red Cross guidance, it was decided to operate once more on my left leg and try to find the reason for it not healing. I could have told them. A teenager needs plenty of good healthy food, loaded with vitamins, milk, fresh vegetables, etc., in order to develop a strong body able to resist and fight off infections.

The surgery this time around was of course under much better conditions than the previous one. I was fully anesthetized by ether, rather than by a fist to the jaw. The surgeons had real instruments and nurses to work with, rather than the rusty scissors and paper bandages that Dr. Lengyel had. The problem remained that my body was not catching up with the time and nourishment that it lost while growing. I did not gain much weight. The draining tubes that were inserted deep under the knee kept draining out the puss, but the body kept on manufacturing it. The hospital and staff tried their best, but the war was still on, and antibiotics were not yet known or available. I remained in the hospital until about the end of February or mid-March (I have great difficulties remembering exact dates), trying to gain weight and strength. I was still unable to put any weight on the left leg. I kept moving around with the support of the crutches.

With time on my hand to think about home, family, and religion, I became more and more anxious to begin the search for the balm that only a home and family could provide. The burden of my thoughts was becoming heavier rather than easier to deal with.

I was not alone in this predicament. There were others like me in the hospital who had a hard time regaining their lost health and strength. The hospital began bringing in some horrific and ghastly cases from other camps, those who survived medical experiments performed on them by Birkenau's infamously notorious Dr. Mengele and his evil cohorts. I remember two young boys from Hungary in particular. One had a section of his skull removed and cancer cells implanted that were still growing on his brain. Another one had a neat square piece of his skin and flesh removed from one of his leg muscles and replaced with a similar square removed from a black man. The implant was infected. The body rejected it and massive infections spread all over his body as a result of that experiment. There were many more horrible cases like those. There was one boy, about my age and of similar background, with whom I became really friendly. I don't recall his name now. He too, like me, was hopping on crutches.

We heard via the hospital "grapevine" that a group of Czech-Jewish partisans had come to Katowice, a very large city about fifty or sixty kilometers from Auschwitz, with a special train to take home all surviving Czech citizens in the area. My friend and I were beginning to plan how we could go there and be repatriated, in spite of our medical conditions. We didn't let anyone else in on our plans to "escape" and try to reach home. We just couldn't wait any longer!

KATOWICE

My friend and I found out that one of the Czech partisans was at the main Auschwitz camp, registering the potential repatriates, to lead them to the train in Katowice. We could not register with them. We were still hospital patients under treatment by the International Red Cross. We didn't have release papers or any sort of identification documents yet, not from the Red Cross, nor from the Russian military Kommandatura, which had overall authority over us. The war was still on, and so was the hunt after fugitive Gestapo and SS men and even Russian deserters. It was a gamble to travel anywhere without proper documentation.

We decided to go A.W.O.L. from the hospital, go to the main camp, and attach ourselves illegally to the transport. We desperately wanted to go home. We made ourselves bundles, packed up into them all the food that we could get our hands on, tied those bundles to our waistbands, and with the crutches in our hands, joined the group. Nobody asked us who we were, or how we got there. The group was made up of survivors from many different camps who did not know each other personally. I guess everyone was busy taking care of themselves and contemplating what awaited them at the end of the journey.

Alas, the train could not come directly into Auschwitz, because many of the railroad bridges between Auschwitz and Katowice were still down from the bombing and sabotaging that went on prior to the Russian occupation. It was decided that the group, several hundred of us, would travel by the electric tramway from Auschwitz till the outskirts of Mislowice. About two to three kilometers outside of town, the tramway halted in the middle of nowhere. The bridge was out. Everyone had to walk a few kilometers from there to the middle of the town, where another tramway was operating into Katowice. It was still terribly cold. The fields were still covered with thick layers of hard packed snow. As a matter of fact, just as we descended from the tramway embankment, several feet above the land level, it started to snow again.

Everyone played "follow-the-leader" from that spot into the town of Mislowice, to board the connecting tram to Katowice. Everyone, that is, those who were able to keep up with the group leader. That did not include the two crippled "fellow-travelers." We were bringing up the rear, hopping along as best as we could. But not quite good enough. We kept falling behind farther and farther. The snow turned into a vicious, wind-driven blizzard! My friend and I could no longer keep pace even with each other. We got separated too. I had no idea where he disappeared to.

It did not take me too long to reach the point of exhaustion. With the wind mercilessly blowing sharp needles of frozen tiny icicles, disguised as snow, into my face and blinding me completely, I got rid of my bundle, hoping to make it easier for me to walk. It did not help. After a few more steps, I was at the end of my stamina. Completely isolated, in the middle of nowhere, I finally gave up trying to continue walking on my one "good" leg. There was no point in even trying anymore. There was no way that I would ever be able to catch up with the group anyway. I just lay down on the tramway embankment, and I began to cry bitterly, from pain and despair. I recited a silent *viduy* (confession of the dying), parts of which I recalled from the Yom Kippur prayers. I entrusted my soul and body to the Creator. I closed my eyes and began to hallucinate about my warm home. The aromas of mother's Shabbat food on the stove... Father saying goodbye to me... Mother, Leitchu, and Yolika calling me to come home...

Suddenly, I felt someone shaking me to wake up. I had no idea how long I was out. I was shivering and screaming and whimpering like a wet dog rescued from an icy pound. When I was finally able to focus my eyes through the frozen tears, I saw a woman with a little boy standing in front of me with a sled laden with firewood. She was talking to me in Polish. I couldn't understand what she was saying. I tried to tell her, in a halting mixture of Czech and Ukrainian that I want to go to Katowice on the electric train. I am sure that she was aware who I was, a sixteen-year-old child in deep distress. She probably also had some feelings of guilt and shame about what by now was common knowledge, what really went on in her immediate vicinity during the Nazi occupation. For whatever reason, she told her boy to off-load the firewood from the sled and stay there to guard it. She motioned for me to climb on the sled and she pulled me in that snowstorm all the way to the tramway station in town! The group had, of course, left by the time I got there.

When I finally arrived in Katowice, the blizzard was unbearable. I struggled against the fierce wind and blinding snow to try to find the gathering place for the repatriates. Once again I became totally helpless. I cried my heart out. I was now convinced that this was the end of my quest for life and home. I asked some passersby to direct me to the camp for refugees. Most of them just shrugged their shoulders and went on. Somebody at long last told me where to go. It took all of my last gasps of strength and stubborn will power to reach the promised warmth and shelter of that camp—any camp for that matter!

The camp was teaming with Russian soldiers and officers who came and went by me as if I was part of the scenery. I got up on my crutches to find shelter. I came to one spot in the camp where I met my conspiratorial friend again. He too had made it at long last. He successfully made the walk from the broken-bridge stop to the station in Mislowice, far behind the rest of the group. No one was aware that we were not with the group, because we were not registered with them. The two of us sat down next to each other and cried. We were scared. We did not see the partisan group leader, or any others from the group, nor any other civilians at all. We were cold and hungry. As we huddled and sobbed, a Russian woman officer approached us.

She asked us in Russian for our papers. We could not produce any. Nor could we explain to her in Russian what we were doing there. She took one good look at us, frightened and confused; she understood who we were. She already knew about Auschwitz. She was among the liberators. Perhaps she was that army doctor who first came into our barrack in Buna... She began to speak to us in Yiddish. She asked us what we were doing here, in this compound. We told her that we want to go home. She almost cried with us. She asked if we were aware of what kind of camp this was. She told us that this was a detention camp for Russian army deserters (there were huge numbers of them all over) and other offenders who were gathered there to be shipped back to Russia, to stand trial and most likely go to Siberia. We were paralyzed with fear. She told us to go into a certain hut in the camp that now served as the camp garage. There we would find an army truck. We should climb into the truck bed and cover ourselves with the tarpaulin that was on it, and she would soon come to take us back to the hospital in Auschwitz.

We did what she told us to do. Soon she showed up in the garage with some hot soup and bread and drove us back to the hospital in the town of Oswiencin. She scolded and admonished us, as any good Jewish mother would, not to attempt another "escape" until the authorities would officially discharge us from the hospital and give us the proper certificates and I.D. papers to travel. We were safe once again! But we were also yearning and dreaming about going home, too. Despair and fear now replaced hope and expectations that were put on hold once again. We remained in that hospital for more treatment, until about mid-April. At that time we were given discharge papers from the Red

Cross and from the hospital officials, requesting safe passage for all of us back to our respective homes.

This time the Russians escorted us to Cracow, another large city in the vicinity of Auschwitz. There we were to wait a few days for another Czech partisan train that would take us back home. The train arrived. The Russian Kommandatura in Cracow issued us I.D. cards as Czech repatriates and official *laissez-passer* documents (temporary international passports). My leg was still draining. I could still not walk on both legs. Crutches were to be my companions for a long time to come. Neither were my spiritual and emotional wounds healing. As time passed and the terrible facts became more clearly focused so did the skepticism and cynicism about the "values" and "truths" that I had been raised to believe in. They no longer made any sense to me. They did not provide me with a rational frame of reference to comprehend the terrible tragedies that befell us. Perhaps, when I got back home, everything would become clearer. My parents would be able to help me see things in their proper perspective. But where was *home*?

Where is Home?

The train was of the exact same type, boxcars, as those which took us to Auschwitz, but with several differences. Our parents were not with us. We were not crowded. The doors were not sealed shut. The small windows were not woven with barbed wire. On the floor were army-type mattresses. At every stop along the way, we were fed by the Russian army, or by the Red Cross, and in some major cities by the "Joint" (American Joint Distribution Committee) branch office in town. We went on a long circuitous journey, because many railroad bridges were still not repaired. The Russians were still fighting the war. They could not stop long enough to rebuild the ruined cities or the country's infrastructure.

We were escorted all the way by a full contingent of Russian officers and soldiers. They were very nice to us but very primitive. They smoked a kind of tobacco root called *machorka*, which they wrapped in newspaper or packaging paper and smoked. Some of the cities we passed on the way were completely wiped out from the fierce fighting that went on there. I don't recall all of their names. I believe that some of them were named Yaslowice, Sanok, and Novy Shanz. Many villages and towns along the way had nothing left standing except for a "forest" of chimneys; the houses were all gone. It was eerie. It was like scenes from a science fiction movie or a defoliated forest.

The trip back took much longer than the trip there. The train had to be rerouted many times and we found ourselves back where we started, after many false starts. We all had very mixed emotions; at least I know that mine were mixed with hope and anxiety. What would happen when I got back to Chust? Whom would I find there? Would my home be waiting for me? Would anyone of my family be there to welcome me? How would I face reality if it turned out to be as I really knew but refused to allow myself to believe it would be? Would I have the will power and the energy to face life alone? I still had no idea of the full extent and the ramifications of what life would be like, or of what radical changes our recent tragic events would bring about in my future.

I wasn't sure that I would be ready for any kind of "normalcy" again. I had seen too much, I had suffered too much to be a "normal" child again. Or worse yet, to be a "grown-up" at age sixteen! I kept changing the bandages of my left leg every day. The wound was not healing. I had to stretch the leg daily to prevent it from forming scar tissue again. The skin or the scar tissue was hurting every day as I kept on tearing it. But I was told to do so before I left the hospital.

After about ten days or so, we finally crossed the border between Poland and Slovakia, at the town of Bardiev, on the first day of May 1945, almost a year after we crossed that border going eastward. The first stop on Czechoslovakian soil was the town of Humane. We could hardly believe our eyes. Here we found a fully organized Jewish community. The local branch office of the Joint gave each of us some civilian clothes, without the traces of the striped material on them. We were put up in a former Jewish school building, with beds, blankets, and even showers for all the returning transports. We were checked over by Czech physicians, given multiple vitamins, and registered by the Joint, which kept track of all the survivors in every large city. We were also given 1,000 cronas (the Czech currency) to spend on ourselves as we pleased. Most of us invaded the town and bought food, candy, and other items that we hadn't seen for a full year. I bought some special foods as I was advised to do by the doctor, in order to build up my strength and gain some weight. I was still emaciated.

The inevitable had happened. The ties to the past had been severed, but nothing was in sight to replace those ties. I was "free," but not happy. I still had some guilt feelings about my newly found freedom. How far would it take me? Who would I be at the end? Would I still be the obedient, shy little boy, stepping forward, one step at a time, only to quickly retreat to the safety of the familiar, comfortable rules and parental guidance that had provided me with security all my life? I felt torn apart inside. The doubts and hesitations became stronger as my options became more numerous and beckoning.

After about a week or two in Humane, the group that had come together disbanded. Everyone went their own way, heading "home." A few of us took a civilian train for the first time in a long while, free of charge (all railroads and buses allowed free passage to all returnees), headed for Chust. We often had to sleep over at the stations' terminal building, on the cement floors. We finally arrived at Kiralyhaz. This was a major hub for trains. From here, after a day or two, we found a train heading in our direction. At long last, I was back in my hometown, *mein shtetle* Chust, once again. I had arrived alone and empty-handed, except for some food and my ever present crutches. Some of my fellow travelers continued for a short while at least to their respective villages in the Chust vicinity. They quickly found out that there was nothing left for them there and came back to the "big city" where a nucleus of a Jewish *kehilah* was in the process of being organized. From the small railroad station, which was closer to our home, I hopped along until I came to the courtyard where we used to live. I came to the door and found that a Gypsy family had taken over our home and all that we left in it as soon as we were deported. They would not let me in. I really didn't put up much of a protest. I was not ready yet, emotionally, to see the inside of what used to be my home, the way it looked now. One of our neighbors, who lived in the same courtyard with us and had been a partisan hidden in the mountains after he ran away from a Hungarian forced-labor battalion, and his wife, were already living back again in their former home. They took me in and gave me a place to sleep. Food was provided by the Joint through a local Jewish committee. I found the hiding place in the cellar where we hid all of our belongings. It was already dug up by someone else and left empty. Mother always suspected that it was one of our neighbors who took the treasure for themselves. I am not so sure. I rather believe that the local non-Jews had a fun time digging up every "suspicious" place, looking for loot, a veritable treasure hunt, soon after we left.

However, I did go back to the woodshed in grandmother's courtyard and dig up the four precious items I had hastily buried there before we were evacuated—the only material connection between the *then* and the *now*. Nothing else of what once belonged to us would ever again be retrieved or restored to us. When mother and Leitchu returned, we divided these items between us. Leitchu took mother's silver candlesticks and father's silver *atara*, both of which were forcefully "liberated" from her, on a train ride, by some Russian soldiers. I took the kiddush cup and the Doxa pocket watch. The watch eventually got broken and lost. But the precious cup is still one of my most prized possessions. This cup was used under the *chupah* of all four of father's grandsons' weddings and on many other family celebrations.

I went out to look around the town. Very few of our friends or acquaintances were to be seen. The war was still on. Many of the concentration camps were yet to be liberated. In the marketplace, in front of our courtyard, I found the peasant women wrapping vegetables and herrings in pages torn out of large volumes of Hebrew books. I clearly saw among them the leather bindings of what once was my father's *Shas* with his name embossed in gold letters on the covers.. I went across the street to explore the *kehilah hoif*. Nothing was the way I had left it. The official *shul* was abandoned and the books strewn all around. In the *kehilah* office only the marble slab with my father's name on it was still there, but nothing else. So where was home? It was gone forever. I was homeless as age sixteen.

Neither was I any longer the person who I used to be before I left home. I was now a complete stranger to my former self. The spiritual transformation from *yeshivah bochur* to one who had no idea of where to go from here was total.

But what to do? The question was both for now as well as for the future, if there was ever to be a future for me.

"ONE FROM A CITY
AND TWO FROM A FAMILY"

...Go and proclaim these words toward the North, and say:
Return, thou backsliding Israel, saith the Lord;
I will not frown upon you;
For I am merciful, saith the Lord.
...Return, O backsliding children, saith the Lord,
For I am a Master unto you,
And I will take you one of a city and two of a family (a clan),
And I will bring you back to Zion.

— Jeremiah 3:12–14

The Prophet was warning the people of the coming destruction. He foresaw that by the time it would all be over, they would be decimated to those pitiful remnants. His prophecy was meant for the sinners of Israel (in the North), as well as for Yehudah in the South, before both were destroyed, during the First Temple period. They were indeed "backsliders"! They served Ba'al and Astoret and the golden calves in Dan and in Bet-El. They probably well deserved their fate. But what kind of backsliding did we do to deserve this kind of fate?! We did not serve idols, nor mistreat our fellow human beings. We were more observant and more learned in the ways of the Torah than any other generation before us! Yet we were decimated to those proportions that Jeremiah predicted! Why? Where did we go wrong? By studying the Torah and the Talmud day and night? By taking care of the basic needs of the poor, the widow, and the orphan? What about all the innocent little children who never knew what life is all about? What about all of the great *tzadikim* and *roshei yeshivah*? All of them were "backsliders," too? What then is the "Path of The Righteous"? ... It just didn't make sense at all. I have always rejected the preaching of some *gedolei hatorah* (the present-day "Sages") that the Holocaust was G-d's retribution for our sins. What absolute nonsense! How dare anyone besmirch the memory of our sainted martyrs who were exterminated for *kiddush Hashem* (sanctifying G-d's name) by referring to them as sinful. Was I more righteous than my little brother, my father, my grandmother? Of course not.

The bitter truth is that the animal instinct is still viable within all of mankind. Sometimes we manage to restrain that jungle law of the survival of the fittest and act civilized for a while. But most of the time, we still act on that primitive instinct: kill and plunder the defenseless! The rest of the world eagerly subscribed that brutal "law" by quietly acquiescing to the wholesale slaughter of innocent human beings without lifting a hand or even a voice to contain those wild and inhuman outrages. The fact that it was the German people who perpetrated these atrocities only verifies that theory. "Civilization" is only a temporary facade, a short-lived experiment. The German "Humanism Kultur" had no firm moral basis that was accepted by its masses. Kant remained a voice in the wilderness. His "pure ethics" theory remained just that, a theory. Nietzsche's dictum rightfully described the German mentality of the survival of the fittest and of the super-race. But in reality any nation in the world whose laws are based on human morality alone (Humanism) is capable of the same kinds of behavior if and when the opportunity and the circumstances come together. The beast comes out of his cave, from time to time, and sheds his masquerade of being more than just a killer with the jungle instinct of the predator.

It is only us, the Jewish people, whose laws are based on morality and on responsibility to a Higher Authority, that have been instilled with the moral code of the Torah, to distinguish between that which is right and that which you can get away with, as a very minor infraction of the general rule. At least this is true for those who have accepted the teachings of the Torah as a way of life. Perhaps that moral code is the thorn in the sides of all those beasts that seek to eliminate us as a pesky thorn, we who constantly preach morality and justice to the nations of the world. Perhaps we make them uncomfortable.

I am still struggling with this question. *Hester panim* (G-d's turning His face from us—abandoning us to our own fate) is just as unacceptable to me as the "sinners" theory. They both have at their core the notion that our martyred loved ones deserved G-d's abandonment and His wrath. They certainly did not. Trying to find an answer to this dilemma has almost literally driven me out of my mind. Hundreds of hours of soul-searching have not given me any relief. I still struggle with the nightmarish images I witnessed. I guess some things are just beyond our capacity to understand. Or perhaps there is nothing to understand. It just happened because people allowed it to happen. Period.

But if there were to be some remnants—where and who were they? It became a daily ritual by most of the returnees, especially the younger ones, like myself, to spend our days at the railroad station, waiting to welcome more survivors. Almost every train brought a few more. We all wanted to hear from them if they had seen or heard about our family members.

When the meager trickle of returnees was interrupted for a while, because of the western front still being engulfed in bitter battles, some of us youngsters, from Chust and from the surrounding villages, decided not to sit around passively, waiting at the train station any longer. We became a "group" or rather a "wolf pack," roaming all over the liberated parts of Europe in a futile search for relatives and fortune, too. We heard that in all capitals of Eastern Europe, the Joint was giving each of the refugees some money to help them reach home and to resume life as best they could. We were on our way to collect that "fortune" from every available source. We traveled together for protection and for planning. We traveled mostly by freight trains, like the veritable hoboes that we had become, rootless and restless bums. At every town there was a free kitchen for meals. We slept on the floors, mostly in or around the train stations. We came to Bratislava, the capital of Slovakia, and collected our money. We went on to Prague and collected there too. We came to Budapest and collected again. Now we traveled through most of Rumania until we reached Bucharest. Again we collected. (We jokingly referred to these payments as our *nadan*, our dowry.) We also cheated a little; we were entitled to a one-time stipend only.

Resentful as we were about what the world had done to us, we never, even for a fleeting moment, entertained the possibility of acts of violence or of revenge. Looting, stealing, rioting, and demolishing property were not in our vocabulary. I guess that some inbred values are there to stay forever. I have never heard of any groups of Holocaust survivors, anywhere in the world, having resorted to such revenge tactics. I suppose that the poet Bialik was right again when he stated: "… and accursed be the one who says: Revenge! For a proper revenge for the blood of even one innocent child—not even Satan himself had yet invented!" Would burning down some houses or smashing the store windows, as many groups who felt unjustly treated by society have done, bring us back any of our loved ones?

Since the Joint authorities became wise to these "double-dipping" practices, they required us to show them an I.D. or some other official documentation before giving out any money. They would stamp the document on the face of it and noted the place and the amount collected. We quickly learned to find a way to outsmart them. Since we had many different documents from different sources, we never submitted more than one document at a time. When we ran out of documents, we just claimed that they were lost or stolen. We had our tattooed arms to prove who we were anyway.

It became a ritual that at every stop along the way, wherever we were traveling and we met new people also wandering from country to country, to read off lists with names of people that someone had heard were alive from any given city in our region. Coming home from Bucharest, my friends and I decided to travel in style. Instead of the freight trains, we would board the very fancy express train from Bucharest to Arrad. Our documents gave us free passage through national borders and on all the freight trains we wanted; however, it did not give us free passage on luxury trains without paying. We tried to avoid the conductor, but he caught up with us. He took our I.D. cards and other valuable documents as "security" so we would go down with him at the next stop to pay the full price. We foolishly let him keep the papers, rather than go with him to pay. We continued on the next freight train on our way back "home."

At the Kiralyhaz station, when I heard one man reading his list of people who were seen on their way home, I heard the words in Yiddish: "Dovid Rosenfeld's *vab mit ihr tochter*" (David Rosenfeld's wife and daughter). I could hardly believe it. I jumped up and questioned the man as to the veracity of his list. When he found out that these were my mother and sister, he told me that they were seen in Prague. I immediately changed my plans. I left the "wolf pack" and took the next train to Prague. At the Joint office there, they verified the fact that my mother and sister were there just a few days ago and were headed toward Budapest. In Budapest, I was told that they left for Bratislava. In Bratislava I was told that they headed to Kosice.

It became clear that they were headed homeward. Instead of chasing them any further, on my crutches, I decided to head back to Chust and pick up the vigil at the train station. In a few days mother and Leitchu arrived. Mother's first words to me were: "Where is father"? I told her that we were separated a long time ago... Mother was understandably very upset and disappointed.

Later on I found out why mother was so upset. She was told at one of those stations along the way, by a first cousin no less, that father and I were both alive and had been seen in Kosice.

The "two from a family" now became three. We each had our little bundles containing all of our possessions. What now? Where do we go from here? Mother immediately took charge of the situation. She was determined to do all that she was able to do with whatever was available to her. The three of us were going to set up a "home" again in Chust and wait for the rest of the family to arrive. We found an abandoned house that used to belong to our friends. It was completely empty, but it had many rooms. We began to gather around us all of our cousins who survived.

We spread out all over town to "organize" mattresses and any pieces of furniture we could find. We also received blankets and some dishes from the Joint office. Mother began to be a "mother" again. Every day we had to go out as scavengers and find useful items to add to the household. Some more relatives came and others left. Our new home became an address and a rest stop for many in need of rest to collect their wits about them before pressing on with their plans to re-establish themselves.

With mother's loving care, and with the opportunity now to rest and gain some weight and strength, plus the assistance of a doctor in town, my wound slowly began to heal. The scar tissue closed up the gaping hole under my knee after the draining tube was removed. Soon I was able to stand and walk on both legs without the support of those dreaded crutches. I felt "whole" again. We stayed in Chust for a while, I can't remember exactly how long, but long enough to become convinced that neither father nor Yolika were ever coming back. We found some photographs of father and of grandmother in the city hall archives that were duplicates submitted when they applied for Hungarian I.D. cards as well as many other official documents.

I found out later that after mother and Leitchu were tattooed with the serial numbers on their arms in Birkenau, they were shipped off to a labor camp in Germany, called Goerlitz, to work in a munitions factory. They worked making canon shells. They, too, like father and I, were sharing what little free time there was together. Sometimes mother got to work in the kitchen and was able to find some extra food to share with Lea. They were also lucky. One of our cousins was appointed *blokelterster* in the adjacent men's camp. As such he had the privilege to come over to the women's camp often. He saw to it that mother and Leitchu got extra food whenever he could. Toward the end of the war, in May or June, the Germans force-marched the entire camp population westward, toward the Allied forces, trying to avoid being captured by the Russians. On the way they shot to death on the spot anyone who could not keep up with the rest of the group. The Germans were in a great hurry. Finally mother and Leitchu became liberated, when their guards left them in the middle of nowhere and they deserted to save themselves.

This arrangement in Chust was great for the immediate needs. But what about the future? This question was soon enough answered by the political events around us, of which we knew nothing.

The Russians Are Coming—Again

We began to hear rumors that Czechoslovakia, under Russian occupation, as was most of Eastern Europe after World war II ended, was being pressured by the Soviets to cede P.K.R. (Ruthenia) to the Soviet Ukraine. They very much wanted to have a firm foothold across those Carpathian Mountains. Apparently they had a hard time battling the retreating Germans over those mountain passes.

To us, who had lived with the Russians for a while now, the "Liberators" turned out to be nothing more than crude and completely undisciplined hordes of thieves, rapists, and even murderers. I will never forget a scene that Leitchu and I saw at the main railroad station in Budapest (Kelety Alomas). There I was with Leitchu waiting for a train to Bratislava. There were a lot of Russian civilians, women and children, also waiting for the train. Russian M.P.'s were keeping a semblance of order in a chaotic terminal. A Russian captain approached one of the M.P. sergeants on the platform, apparently demanding some preferential treatment on the waiting line for a relative or a friend. Soon they were arguing quite loudly. Suddenly, the sergeant pulled out his pistol and shot the captain in the head at point blank range! A chase and gun battle ensued in the station and along the parked trains, until the sergeant, too, was shot. We were all scrambling for cover and screaming in terror.

Scenes like these and what we had heard about the rudeness of the soldiers made it quite clear to most of the Jews who came back to Carpatho-Russ that we did not want to remain there and become Russian citizens. But where would we go?

When the Czechoslovak authorities suddenly offered all the inhabitants of Carpathia the opportunity to "opt" for Czech citizenship, we knew for sure that the Russians were taking over. Only people of voting age could opt for citizenship. Mother went to acquire the necessary documents. I don't recall if Leitchu had already reached the age for voting or not. I could not vote or "opt" for myself, since I was still a minor. In theory, we assumed, I was "covered" by mother's status. (This assumption cost me dearly later on.)

It was time to pack up the bundles once again and look for a place to settle down and call "home." Many people, especially those who had come home immediately when the war was over in Czechoslovakia, or those who were hiding in the forests with the partisans, were encouraged by the government to move westward into what was once called the Sudetenland (Sudetengebit in German). This was the most industrialized region of the country. Almost all of the population of this region were ethnic Germans and actively took part in dismembering the republic in 1938. They were all traitors to the Czechs, who treated them with utmost respect as a fully autonomous minority. Now, after the war, the highly democratic Czech government decided to get rid of this "fifth column." There was an immediate mass transfer of that entire German population back into Germany. They were given a half hour for each family, to pack up their essential belongings and board the military trucks and buses, for the ride across the border into Germany, to be reunited with their kinfolk. There were no protests from the United Nations or from any other "do-gooders." Before anybody could organize "human rights" marches, the transfer of almost four million Germans was completed.

There were now thousands of homes and businesses, filled with everything, abandoned and available for the taking. You just reported to the authorities that you are now the new owner of this or that home, store, or factory. Among those who went up to those free areas were some of our friends and relatives who got there in time to take over some prime properties.

In the meantime, while we were waiting for the new citizenship papers to arrive, and trying to decide what to do next, Leitchu and I were recruited by a relative, who had lived with us in Chust to learn wig-making from mother and now lived in Bratislava, to smuggle large quantities of American cigarettes across the borders from Czechoslovakia to Hungary. There was good money in it. Except when you got caught by the authorities or robbed by the Russian soldiers on the trains.

Finally we decided to move away from Chust and find a place in Sudetenland. Leitchu and I were on our way to find a place to take over. We had low priority. Former soldiers, partisans, and political prisoners had first choice. On the train between Bratislava and Prague, tragedy struck me again. I was sitting on the steps of the crowded passenger train with the door wide open. Suddenly, a freight train came, on the parallel tracks, from the opposite direction. Something stuck out from the freight train that slammed the door with great force, hitting my very vulnerable left leg. I was in great pain. By the time we reached Prague, I was again burning with very high fever and unable to use my injured leg. With Leitchu's assistance I hopped to the nearest hotel.

Leitchu realized that the fever was a bad sign. She phoned for an ambulance. I was taken to the Divishova Clinika Hospital on Sept. 3, 1945. I pleaded with Leitchu and with the doctors not to operate. I could not survive surgery again. But it was decided to go ahead anyway. Again I cried and begged not to put me to sleep with ether. The horrible hallucinations of floating in midair from the ether given to me at the second operation on my leg in the civilian hospital in Oswiencin were still vivid in my feverish mind. We bribed the doctor with a few packs of cigarettes (the most prized currency). He promised not to use ether. He lied, of course. I was in the hospital till Sept. 12, and continued as an outpatient for a few weeks after that.

I recall the agony as the ether slowly, very slowly, began to knock me out. And I had the terrifying feeling of floating and sinking free-fall into a bottomless abyss. Although my hands were tied down to the operating table, with my fingers I tore the pockets of the surgeon's white coat. This time the surgeon cut high up on my thigh, rather than under the knee. A draining tube was inserted once again. After I was discharged from the hospital and spent a few weeks as an outpatient, we were on our way. I was on crutches again. We were attempting to find a place for the family (the three of us) to settle in. (Several years later, I wrote to the Divishova Clinika for an official transcript of my hospital stay, and on June 1964 I received a transcript and a very touching note from the surgeon.)

For the first time I found out what that stubborn infection was that had lasted for such a long time. The transcript states: "The patient had phlegmonous inflammation of his left thigh while a prisoner at the Auschwitz concentration camp. Now he was admitted with a recurrent abscess at the inner side of his left thigh. On Sept. 4, 1945, an incision and drainage was performed. The causative organism was found to be Beta-Hemolytic Streptococcus and Pneumococcus."

Alas, by the time we arrived in Sudetenland, all was taken. At first we came to the large industrial city of Liberec, since one of mother's close childhood friends got there in time to set up house in a very beautiful and large villa. We stayed with her for a little while. Then we rented two rooms from a squatter who served in the Czech army. After a while, we decided to accept an invitation from our cousins to move near them in Usti-nad-Labem, another large industrial city in Sudetenland. They had taken over a large farm from a transferred German family. They raised cattle and hogs and various kinds of crops. We rented part of an apartment from a former partisan. We now decided to stay there since that partisan also had taken over a farm in nearby Nestedice; we had the whole apartment in Usti to ourselves.

In time, we even took in a boarder, who was a master watchmaker. We set up a home in Usti. We also spent a lot of time in Nestedice on the farm. Although both of these cousins were very observant people before the war, they, like most of us, were plagued by unanswerable questions about the horrors of the Holocaust. They had deliberately given up any pretense of living by the rules of the past. The past was all a big lie, a farce, and a pretense. They raised and ate pigs on that farm. I helped out on the farm. I drove teams of horses hitched to wagons, full of fertilizer from the stables and from the compost heaps to the fields. I took the cows to be fertilized, too, over mother's strenuous protests that I was too young for such experiences. I got a real "education" there....

In Usti, we settled down to an almost "normal" lifestyle. There were a few other families like us who had fled from the clutches of the Soviets. A *shul* was organized by some of the more senior members of the new *kehilah* in Usti. Interestingly, it seems that the older the survivors were the less rebellious they were and more eager to return, as quickly as possible, to a modicum of "normalcy." However, we were a group of a few younger boys and girls who just rejected that normalcy. We were more or less like the Israelites at the time of Eliyahu and Achav, "hopping between two branches of the tree" (serving G-d and Baal at the same time). Because of the wishes of those of our elders who were eager to re-establish life according to tradition, we came to *shul*; we observed, at least publicly, the Shabbat and the holidays.

Yet as time went on and the news of the Zionist efforts to establish a State in Palestine reached us, we decided to organize ourselves into a Zionist youth organization. We began to teach ourselves Hebrew (and Esperanto). For some reason, which only trained professionals might be able to figure out, we decided to become a branch or "nest" of Bnei Akiva—the Mizrachi youth movement, a totally religious organization! We even organized our own *minyan* and wore our special uniforms. Yet we continued with our "double lives" when we were away from home. Apparently, the "spark" was still not completely extinguished. Sure there was rebellion, but there was also nostalgia for the firm foundations and practices that gave us a link to the past and a sense of continuity.

The National Bachad (Religious Pioneers Movement) with headquarters both in Prague and in Bratislava provided our branch members with *tefilin* and *sifrei kodesh*. We began to have *shiurim* on Torah, Navi, and Talmud. Ever so slowly, we found ourselves being "converted" back to our original roots. We gave up the "freedoms" of doing as we pleased in an attempt to show our ability to be independent. Going to Bnei Akiva summer camp helped in the transformation process, too. None of us would ever go back all the way to the Hasidic manner of lifestyle. We have discovered that there is a "sane" Orthodox way of Judaism, which does not reject the realities of life, but rather incorporates them into a sensible practice of authentic Yiddishkeit.

This new awareness would eventually take almost all of our group members back to a total commitment to a Torah way of life in spite of the open wounds and unanswered painful questions. It would be a much stronger commitment than ever before. We had truly come full circle. We had seen and experienced the other way. It was void of lasting values to hold on to. It did not offer any answers or balm for the deep lesions in our hearts, souls, and minds.

Early in 1946, there was a large gathering of the European section of the World Zionist Organization held in the magnificently beautiful Hotel Poop in Karlovy Vary (Karlsbad), one the most famous resort and spa cities in all of Europe. Our whole group decided to go there and be part of that historic

147

conference. Since we could not afford hotel accommodations, we found an attic with straw "mattresses" available for rent. We took most of the food along from home. It was very exciting. All the leaders of the Zionist movement were there. Most meetings and plenary sessions were open to the public, so we went to listen. Just mingling among the "big-shots" in that beautiful hotel was a great experience.

During my frequent visits to Prague, I always made it a point to pray at the world famous and historic Alt-Neu (Old-New) synagogue. It was the oldest actively used synagogue in all of Europe. It was the place of worship of the famed Maharal of Prague, the creator and master of the Golem. No, I never found enough courage to go up into the attic to see if the Golem was still resting up there. Neither did anyone else. The whole Jewish Ghetto of ancient Prague was a most fascinating place. The Old Jewish cemetery, perhaps over a thousand years old, had graves and headstones six to twelve layers on top of each other. The Jewish community office building had its famous clock with Hebrew letters on the face instead of numbers and hands that rotate from right to left, the Jewish way, rather than the usual "clockwise." The ancient and majestic Karlovy Most (Karl's Bridge), spanning the Vltava River with its magnificent statues, among them the heart-rending massive crucifix emblazoned with huge Hebrew words, "*Kadosh, Kadosh, Kadosh, Hashem Tzevaot*" (Holy, Holy, Holy, the Lord of Hosts). I miss Prague to this day. In my estimation it is the most beautiful city in the world, second only to Jerusalem, of course.

In Usti, mother began earning a good living for us. She was again making wigs. She would travel to Prague and order the wigs, set them, and sell them to the women who once again got married and wished to continue with the old lifestyle. When we first came to Usti, mother recalled the name and address of a large wig materials wholesale firm that she used to buy from before the war.

I went to Prague with her, since she didn't speak any Czech at all. Lo and behold, they found her account sheet. They immediately re-established for her an unlimited line of credit, since we had no money to pay for anything. They also put her in touch with a wig-making salon that offered to provide her with their facilities and with a credit line. Mother was now able to take orders from the women in Usti and in Prague, buy the needed materials, have the workers to make them and the facilities to fashion them to the precise specifications of her customers. It gave her a new sense of achievement as a provider for her family.

Mother now often traveled by herself to Prague to place her orders (most of the merchants spoke German, if absolutely necessary), and to pick up the finished products. One evening, she had not returned home to Usti as she had planned to do. We assumed that she missed her train (a trip of about an hour and a half). However, when she failed to arrive the following two days, we became terrified that something has happened to her. I went to Prague to try and find out what the problem was. I had no idea where to begin the search. I decided to go to the Joint office in Prague. They had no idea where she might be. Then I went to the *kehilah* office. There, one of the officials was one of our friends from Chust. They began an inquiry of her whereabouts. They called all the hospitals. No one had a record of such a person. But when they called the police headquarters, we were told that she was being held in prison! We had no idea why she was arrested. I was finally able to post a bond for her and have her released. Apparently she had to remain in Prague overnight. The law required all people from out of town to register at the local police station, indicating where they will be staying and the reason for the visit. Since mother didn't speak the language or know the law, she failed to register. She did not have her citizenship papers or any other I.D.'s on her. She was arrested when the hotel clerk reported that she came without papers and did not register with the police. She never again traveled without the proper documents.

I became very involved in the Bnei Akiva activities. I was now teaching modern Hebrew to groups of members, at age seventeen. It seems that I had retained a great deal of the *lashon kodesh* (the holy tongue), from my *cheder* and yeshivah days, to convert it with the aid of a little grammar book into the modern *Ivrit*.

The Zionist ideal of rebuilding a destroyed land has also become an important ingredient in my own rebirth and rehabilitation. It provided me with an outlet for my need to learn and discover new ideas and different modes of life to replace the one I had rejected. After long arguments and even fights with my mother, I decided to join a few of my new friends in the adventure of going on *hachshara*, a pioneer training experience in preparation for life on a kibbutz in Israel. I had decided that that was what I must do. Mother tried every argument to keep me from going away. But something was driving me. I was restless. Perhaps the idea of becoming a *chalutz* in Israel was the coup-de-grace for purging myself of the anti-Zionist philosophy and indoctrination of Satmar and the price we paid for adhering to it.

I decided to go.

HACHSHARA, PRISON, AND PARIS

After saying our tearful goodbyes, my friends and I took the train to Prague. There we joined another group and were on our way to Michalovce, a small town in Eastern Slovakia. There, in a large house that once belonged to a wealthy Jewish family, a *kibbutz hachshara* (preparatory farm) of the Hapoel Hadati (the religious worker) was set up. The girls were housed upstairs and the boys downstairs. We had two married couples with children as our house parents.

There was a study hall and a *shul* in a smaller building on the grounds. We studied Hebrew and the history of the founders of religious Zionism. We learned about life in Palestine. A special *shaliach* from Tirat Tzvi kibbutz came for a few weeks to indoctrinate us. There were also regular Torah and Talmud *shiurim*. We all ate together and sang patriotic songs. On Motzei Shabbat, we would have a *medurah* (bonfire) in the backyard and sit around it to hear stories of the great Zionist leaders, past and present.

Since *hachshara* literally means preparation or getting ready, we had to find some work that would be useful and productive in a kibbutz. Some of us, about ten or twelve boys, found ourselves working in a saw mill and ceramic factory. Others found work on farms. We worked very hard. We were making all kinds of wood products, boards, plywood, broom and ax handles, as well as ceramic floor tiles. All of our earnings were pooled together to pay for food and for all other expenses. The spirit and the camaraderie were high. We finally found some purpose in life and an extended "family." There were about forty or so members in our group, mostly young kids orphaned and alone in the world. We now had a goal and a future to look forward to, and to plan for. We had also found a channel for the values that we had been raised upon and for the religious practices of our former lives. We were excited about establishing our own *garin* (nucleus) for a separate religious kibbutz in Palestine. We were going as soon as we were really ready and as soon as they would be able to get the logistics in place to circumvent the British blockade around Palestine.

Michalovce was once a very active Jewish community. Now there were only a handful of survivors. The owner of the saw mill where I worked was one of those survivors. He treated us like a father. They had managed to create a small *kehilah* again. We were "adopted" by them. We realized that now we were not alone anymore after all. The main revelation to me was the realization of two very important lessons. First, that you can be observant and totally religious even if you still had not found satisfactory answers to the gnawing and pestering questions. And second, that there is a great wide world of Judaism that is not based on ignorance and on superstitions. Satmar was neither the authentic nor the only mode of expressing strong adherence to Torah and *mitzvot*. These two "revelations" formed the pattern and paved the road to my full return to Hashem, by way of my commitment to eventually study in a great *Litvishe* (non-Hasidic) yeshivah, and the study of Jewish History, Hebrew literature, *dikduk* (grammar), Poetry, and Philosophy at a future date. My adherence to *"Torat Yisrael, Am Yisrael,* and *Eretz Yisrael"* (The Torah, the People, and the Land of Israel are one) and total commitment to these principles have saved me from the clutches of oblivion. My future life revolved around these basic believes: You can be a complete Jew even if you have questions; you may question as long as your beliefs and practices do not hinge on finding satisfactory answers. And most importantly, there is tranquility and peace of mind that comes with being committed to a set of everlasting values and practices. Satmar is not the only way. Not for me, anyway.

Things in Michalovce were going great. Stability, companionship of friends, and a new way of life seemed to be the precise prescription for what tormented me. I got to meet most if not all of the leaders of the World Mizrachi Organization, e.g., Moshe Shapiro (later the perpetual minister of the Interior of Israel), Dr. Yosef Burg (Minister of the Interior and of Religions), Shlomo Zalman Shragai (Mayor of Yerushalayim), among many others. I did feel some guilt about having left mother alone in Usti. But I was too young to really understand her feelings; after all she was still living in the past, while I was busily planning for my future and my own emancipation from the bondage of the past.

In Yiddish the expression goes: "*Der mench tracht – and G-t lacht*" (loosely translated: Man plans, G-d laughs). While we were busy working, so too were the fiendish bureaucrats and leaders of the rabid anti-Semitic Slovak government, the followers of the executed war criminal Monsignor Tisso. They were plotting and scheming of how to rid themselves of the influx of more Jews, mostly from Carpathia.

One day, as I was busily working in the saw mill, with my leather boots and fatigue-style work clothes, two Slovak gendarmes approached me and asked my name. After checking their list, they put me in handcuffs and arrested me. They did the same to a few others in the work yard. We were not told the reason for the arrest, nor what we were charged with. We were very rudely tossed on an open truck and taken to the jail in the basement of the local police station. When we got there, we found that other members of our kibbutz, who worked in other places, were there too. We were put in two big holding cells, boys in one and girls in the other. There must have been about eighteen to twenty of us altogether. Our suspicions about the reason for our arrest became clearer to us when we realized that all of us in prison were from

Carpathia. None of the Slovak members of our kibbutz were arrested with us.

As soon as the *kehilah* found out about what happened, they hired an attorney to find out what was going on. When the local lawyer was unable to find out anything, the Mizrachi office in Bratislava made contact with the police officials there. They, too, refused to tell anyone anything. Finally, the Prague office of the Joint and the Jewish Agency were told that the Russian authorities, who were still occupying Czechoslovakia, had demanded that all former Russian "deserters" must be returned to Russia to face desertion charges (and presumably Siberia). The more-than-eager Slovak gendarmerie, in their zeal to get rid of us, included all of the former Carpathian inhabitants as deserters from Russia, even though it was obvious that the Russians were only after their own army deserters. The fact that we had officially opted for and were granted Czech citizenship did not matter to them at all, especially since we did not have our own citizenship papers to prove that fact (since we were all minors and were not issued our own opting certificates).

The people in Prague were unable to do anything for us. The Interior Ministry, that had control over citizenship and over the police, claimed that since Slovakia was an autonomous region, only they could decide what to do in this case. The Jewish organizations in Bratislava hired a whole battery of high-powered lawyers to represent us. Alas, to no avail. A large amount of bribe money (millions of cronas) was offered to the chief of police to let us go. Nothing moved them. We were once again locked up in a prison, not for committing any crimes, but for being "undesirable Jews" in an anti-Semitic environment. We were horrified of the prospect of winding up in a prison camp somewhere in remote Siberia. We cried a lot. We were all still very young kids, sixteen to eighteen years old. We were trapped, again.

The police did permit the Slovak citizens of our kibbutz to bring us kosher food. We were becoming desperate. We also did not smell too good after being deprived of washing, changing clothes, and showering for five days. On Shabbat morning a truck pulled up in the prison yard. We were loaded into the truck, crying and screaming. They were taking us to the Russian border, about thirty kilometers to the east, just outside Uzhorod (Ungvar), the former capital city of Carpathia, to hand us over to the Russian military authorities.

News of what was now happening to us quickly spread and it reached the leaders of the Michalovce Jewish *kehilah*. Everyone, young and old, left the synagogues. It was Shavuot, if my memory is correct, and they all came running to the police station prison. They pleaded with the chief to give them a few more days to obtain the proper documents from Prague. It did not help. The police became abusive in their manner toward the Jewish leaders and the lawyers, their anti-Semitic venom spewing. A bribe was offered by the owner of the saw mill where most of us worked, Mr. Shoenberger, to the civilian driver of the Jewish-owned truck, to fake mechanical problems with the vehicle to allow them some more time. He, too, was arrested and charged with interfering in a police operation.

In desperation, two young ladies lied down on the pavement in front of the truck, in an attempt to block its way out from the police station. While they were being physically removed from blocking the way, one of our Slovak kibbutz members (Yitzchak Friedman) ran across the street to a butcher shop and grabbed a large knife, attempting to cut the tires of the truck. He was brutally beaten up by the police, arrested, and charged with attempted murder of the police chief. Now the truck was completely surrounded by the crowd of Jews. The police had no way to move us. We were taken back into our cells.

A few hours later, we were once again loaded into the truck (with fixed tires). However, the scene in front of the police station was a shocking throwback to the horrors of the Gestapo days.

The entire main street, for as far as we could see from the truck, was lined on both sides with policemen and soldiers, with their automatic submachine guns at the ready, spaced no more than a few feet apart from each other. They formed an effective wall between us and the crowd of helpless Jewish onlookers.

We were on our way again, this time without any interference. The truck did not stop until we reached the fence and barriers on the Slovak side of the border with Russia (Ukraine). A signal was sent to the Russian border guards across "no-man's land" to summon the officer in charge. Meantime, while we were waiting for the Russian commander, we slumped exhausted into the bed of the truck and cried bitterly. I was sure that I would never see mother again. I was again panic-stricken. We were huddled together and shivered with fear. The police escort called us all kinds of dirty names. We were beaten to make us stand up and to stop crying before the Russians came. They told us that they would finish the job of ridding Slovakia of its Jews, which Tisso and Hitler had begun. One officer demanded and confiscated my boots. He told me that I wouldn't need them anymore where I was going. Soon carloads of *kehilah* functionaries and lawyers arrived at the border. They, too, were beaten up and scolded by the police chief. He threatened to include them all among us deserters and send them off to Siberia.

The coincidence of the dates added to my feelings of utter despair. It was Shavuot again. Just a mere three years had passed since we arrived in Auschwitz under almost similarly cruel conditions on the same date; we were once again facing oblivion! History, indeed, repeats itself.

After a while, a Russian command car arrived across the border. The Russian officer, a full colonel, took a good look at us as we were standing there in the truck sobbing bitterly. He then told us almost in a whisper, in perfect Yiddish: "*Weint nit kinderlech, es vet sein gut*" (don't cry children, it will be good). To us he was an angel of mercy sent by our martyred loved ones to save us. The colonel told the crest-fallen chief of police that he was sorry, but that he couldn't accept us since he had no official orders from his headquarters to accept us, since we obviously were not military deserters. He advised the chief to make the proper applications through the Soviet embassy and when he would get an official deportation order, he would take us to the holding camp outside Prague, from where Russian civilian *émigrés* were being "repatriated" to Russia.

Needless to say everyone, except for the miserable police chief, was delighted to have gained additional time. We were brought back to the same prison cells from where we left. That whole affair took almost the entire day. We were very hungry and exhausted, physically and emotionally drained from the day's events.

After a few more days of lobbying the authorities, both in Bratislava and in Prague, without any success (everyone was scared of the Russians), the police chief once again set the time for our deportation to Russia, this time with the proper authorization for the transfer. For some vicious reason, he once again chose Shabbat as the deportation day!

Except that this time, while the Jewish "establishment" and the well-intentioned Czech officials gave up on trying to help us, the Zionist youth movement, and especially the Mizrachi and Hapoel Hamizrachi youth organizations went into action. They put a rescue plan in motion. In one of the loaves of bread that our kibbutz members were allowed to bring us, we found a few steel-cutting blades and a note with instructions to be ready for a bold and daring escape at midnight on Friday. I got to keep the saw blades in my tall boots, which I recovered from the policeman. We were very excited and worried at the same time. What if something would go wrong?

Nevertheless when Friday came, we were ready. All of the Zionist youth groups in the entire region, from the extreme right to the extreme left, formed a "rescue army"; some actually carried loaded pistols. Since it was late at night, there was only one guard on duty. One of the fellows and a couple of the girls brought a bottle of good Vodka to the prison office and began drinking with the guard until he fell asleep, drunk. We were also quite lucky that night. While the drinking went on in the outer guard room, we began sawing away at the bars of the windows. We stood on each other's shoulders, to reach the high window, and took turns sawing. The girls did the same in their cell.

The noise of the sawing was drowned out by an unusually heavy downpour accompanied by thunder and lightning. We coordinated the heavy noises with the thundering. Precisely at midnight, our friends on the outside arrived. By now the bars were cut and bent out of place. We climbed on each other's shoulders, the short ones on the shoulders of the taller ones, into the helping arms of our rescuers. Only the last one of the group had to have help to be pulled up from the deep basement through the very narrow opening in the high window. We were now all out in the harsh, cold, wonderful, and free outdoors. We were soaked to the bones in the heavy downpour.

Our rescuers posted guards and led us, one at a time, with pistols in hand, to a waiting truck that was hidden behind some tall bushes. We climbed in and covered ourselves with the heavy tarpaulins. Before long we arrived to the outskirts of Kosice, a large town about forty kilometers away. We stopped at a deep ravine along the highway. We hid in the wet ravine while our friends continued into town to see if the police were already searching for us. Soon they returned with the good news that all seems to be quiet and normal. We were driven to the *miha* (a children's home and orphanage, under Mizrachi sponsorship). We changed into warm, dry, clothes and were given food. We rested there for a few days, hidden from everyone, until it would be ascertained what was happening back in Michalovce. After a few days, we were given false identity papers and traveled separately but on the same train to Prague. The police checked everyone's papers several times, but they did not have pictures of us. No "mug shots" of us were ever taken! In Prague we immediately got new identities, once again. This time they were not Czech I.D.'s, but International Red Cross *laissez-passer* documents identifying us as surviving Polish Jewish refugees, traveling through Czechoslovakia on our way to Palestine. I think that my name became Jerzy Grossman, thirty-two years old, from Lodz. Within a few hours (I didn't even have time to get in touch with mother by phone—we were not permitted to do so for security reasons), we joined a transport of Polish refugees traveling through Prague, in a long freight train, on their way to Paris, Marseilles, and Israel!

From Paris I wrote mother a very long letter, telling her what we went through in the past three weeks. She had no idea that I was no longer in the *hachshara* in Michalovce. She was naturally shocked. The three of us were now separated, once again. Mother and Lea in Usti, and I in Paris.

In 1986, we participated in the annual gathering of former Czechoslovak Bachad members in Nir Etzion, Israel. There, I met many members of our former kibbutz in Michalovce. From a special book of memoirs and history of the movement, I found out that after we had escaped from prison, the leaders of the Jewish community brought the police chief to trial for his anti-Semitic actions in our case. He was dismissed from his high position and the whole affair was dropped from the record. We no longer had to be afraid of the Czech or the Slovak police. Of course, we had no idea at that time of the turn of events in Michalovce.

In Paris, we were greeted as heroes. It seems that the story of our plight in Michalovce traveled far through the *shlichim* (emissaries) of the Haganah and Bricha (the Zionist Organization's rescue and "illegal" *aliyah* network). We were taken to a Bachad

Kibbutz, very similar to the one we had just left in such a hurry. It was a large mansion, surrounded by a very high stone fence that once belonged to a Jewish family that did not survive the war. It was located in a resort village, L'Isle Adam, in the Seine-et-Oise region about twenty to twenty-five kilometers north of Paris. Here, too, we carried on with the same routine of learning and preparing ourselves for *aliyah*. Except that we did not go to work at all. We were mere transients, waiting for the right conditions to move down south to Marseilles and into ships to Palestine, or to Cyprus, if the British navy would catch us on the high seas.

Since I had all that free time on my hands now, I began once more to try to understand what had happened to us in general and to me in particular. It did me no good. I was again plagued by nightmares. I would wake up startled in the middle of the night, drenched with perspiration and panic. Almost every night I dreamed of seeing and talking with my father. I would plead with him to come with me, to let mother and Leitchu know that he is alive. I kept asking him how he can stand it, to let us suffer so much and mourn for him needlessly. Sometimes I would see myself, in the dream, behind the barbed wires of Buna again. I would scream out in agony: how did I wind up in here once again? Had I not sworn that I would never be taken alive into concentration camps, again?

The restless nights brought with them fatigue, loss of appetite, and melancholy during the day. The kibbutz's house-parents (a Jewish-French family) took me to see a doctor. He injected me with massive doses of vitamins directly into my arteries (or veins). He also gave me liver injections; I had to drink ox blood, all in an effort to build up my very frail physical condition. This was done on a regular basis for several months. It did not help much. My doubts about justice and fairness came back to haunt me again. Since I was a member of a religious kibbutz, I lived as an Orthodox and fully observant Jew.

160

The fact that mother kept writing and telling me how miserable she was without me and that G-d didn't save my life only to lose it on the battlefields of Palestine did not perk me up. It just added to my general state of upheaval and restlessness. I couldn't cope with all of the problems that had befallen me.

Under the massive pressures, I gave in to mother. I agreed to come home as soon as I got a copy of my Czech citizenship paper and obtained a passport. Mother immediately set out to work on it. In the meantime, the time had come for my group to move on south to embark on the trip to Palestine. Using the excuse that I was still under medical treatment, I said goodbye to my friends and told them that I would catch up with them soon in Palestine, on the next transport. The kibbutz allowed me to stay on. I would now travel almost daily to Paris to explore and to enjoy the magnificent sights of the City of Lights. Mother sent me some money (U.S. dollars) in letters, as did my very poor uncle from Queens. After a while, the kibbutz and the Bachad office in Paris realized that I was no longer interested in *aliyah*. I had to move out of the kibbutz. I rented a small room in the village from a non-Jewish family.

After spending about a year in France, I finally received my documents from mother and obtained a passport from the Czech Embassy in Paris, valid only for one trip back home. I was on my way back "home," to Usti again. I made the trip back to Usti by civilian train! As we passed over German territory, I fasted the whole the time and I refused to set foot on German soil at the numerous stops along the journey (I have never set foot on German soil, nor do I ever want to). It was with mixed feelings and great concern for my future that I arrived back "home."

I continued with the medical treatments of vitamins and liver injections that I began in Paris, because I still was very thin, almost feeble. The time had come to make plans for the future. Rumors were ripe again that the Communist Party and the Russians would soon be taking over the only true democracy still left in Eastern Europe, Czechoslovakia. Everyone began making arrangements to leave Czechoslovakia, either for America or for Palestine. Since there was fighting going on now in 1947 in Palestine, mother and I were applying for entry visas to America. This was a long and tedious process. You had to wait for a quota number. This sometimes took years of waiting. Even the fact that mother had a brother, a U.S. citizen, who sent her an "affidavit" (a sort of guaranty that we will not become a public burden). Leitchu was making plans to leave soon for Switzerland.

In the meantime, I began to observe our boarder, as he was fixing watches at home. I decided to become a watchmaker, too. This was a very difficult task for me. Since childhood, I had almost no vision in my right eye (20 x 600), which is not a very suitable situation for such tedious and precise work as watchmaking. But I kept on trying, even though I was convinced that I would never be good enough to make my living from it. There was not much else to do. Most of my friends had, by then, left town. Most of them went to Czech military training camps as a preparation for *aliyah* and for fighting in Palestine, by a special arrangement worked out between the Jewish Agency and Jan Masaryk, the Czech foreign minister at that time. He was one of the most humane and great leaders of Czechoslovakia, a worthy son of his great father.

The Communists became ever bolder. They armed all the factory workers and organized them into militias. Daily demonstrations and marches by the Communists left no doubt that soon they would take over. We had to make immediate plans to leave the country, especially I, who, because of my age would soon be drafted into military service.

One of my cousins was already in America. He was part of a youth transport from the D.P. camps of Germany, who received special, non-quota visas as yeshivah students to come to America to continue their studies. He was now a full-time high school student at Mesivta Torah Vodaas in the Williamsburg section Brooklyn. He succeeded in convincing the yeshivah registrar that I was a yeshivah boy who wants nothing else in life but to continue with his studies. They sent me a certificate of acceptance as a regular full-time student. The American Consulate in Prague would grant me a visa, even though they were quite aware of the fact that I was not attending the only yeshivah in Czechoslovakia established in Frantishkove Lazne (Francesbad), under the leadership of a Rabbi Forhand (although I was registered there). My attire and appearance were not those of a bona-fide yeshivah student. They knew very well that this was a "legal fiction," designed to bypass the quota system with the sole objective to get as many young boys out of the country as possible before the Iron Curtain would descend and swallow up this democracy, too.

However, getting a Czech passport and exit visa turned out to be a much tougher task. I had to get all kinds of certificates and affidavits, from the Ministry of Education, from the Police and from the Ministry of the Interior. Finally, I received the coveted passport. However, to my chagrin, when I went to the U.S. Consulate to pick up my student visa, it was discovered that under the entry "profession" the passport stated "watchmaker" instead of "student." They could not grant me a student visa under these circumstances. I can't figure it out to this day what went wrong. How did this happen? I couldn't have been that stupid! Most likely, in my police I.D. papers it was important to have some occupation listed, otherwise you were considered a vagrant and a parasite on society.

My dear sister came to the rescue. She did some research and found out the current address of the former Czech school principal in Chust, who was now retired somewhere in rural Moravia. She went to see him. She spoke fluent Czech, which I didn't. Therefore, it was best that she went by herself. She persuaded him to write me a letter stating that he remembered me as a high school student of great promise, and that I should be afforded the opportunity to continue with my studies on a higher level. We went back to the Ministry of Education to certify the legitimacy of the principal having served in Chust before the war. Armed with those documents, we returned to the Ministry of the Interior to get a new passport with the correct designation on it as a student. The only thing they were willing to do for me was to put in an official correction in the existing passport. This was of no help at all.

Leitchu did not give up. Daily she went from one level of bureaucrat to the next highest, with the same sob story. Finally she succeeded in touching the heart of a sympathetic official, and a new passport with the correct entries was issued. Our happiness was complete. The Consulate issued me a student visa, outside the quota roster, valid for one year only. I had to pledge that after the year of studies, when I would become an ordained rabbi, I would return to Czechoslovakia to serve as a rabbi. This was the basis and the rationale for the passport and for the visa.

Then I had to bring a doctor's certificate that I was healthy. It had to come from a physician officially designated and appointed by the U.S. Consulate. I passed. I did not suffer from any contagious diseases. Getting together enough money to purchase train and ship passage was no easy task either. But mother came up with the needed funds. Now we had to wait for the Czech exit visa, as well as for transit visas from Germany, from the Allied occupying forces in Germany, and from the French Embassy. While we were running around in Prague from one office to the next, we watched the daily marches of the armed civilian "worker's militia" and the slogans and posters demanding the resignation of the Social-Democrat government in favor of a coalition government headed by the Worker's Party.

My exit visa and all other transit visas were coordinated for a departure date at the end of May 1948. While I was waiting for that day, an upheaval occurred. In February 1948 (I don't remember the exact date), the radio announced with great "sadness" that Jan Masaryk, the Foreign Minister of the coalition government headed by the Communist Gottwald, committed suicide by jumping out of the window of his office. Nothing could have been further from the truth! The few newspapers that were still free of government control reported that a small caliber gunshot wound was found behind the ear of the Minister. Everyone knew that he was executed by his Communist overlords. He would have never committed suicide. Everyone who knew him knew that he was an upbeat kind of bachelor who enjoyed life. He always mingled with the plain folk. He rode the public buses and often walked unescorted on the streets.

It took only a few weeks for the Communists to stage a "putsch" with the help of their militia, and take over the entire government and the army which was composed of some elements that served in the British Eight Army as a Czech component, and others who served with the Russian army, under General Svoboda, during the war.

We were very frightened that soon the borders would be closed shut by the Iron Curtain and no one would be permitted to leave the country, as was the case in all other "satellite" states. It was my good fortune that the Communists had a hard time in subduing and subjugating the proud and traditionally democratic Republic. When the time for my departure came, we said our very sad goodbyes, again, and I left with a heavy heart, not knowing what awaited me once I would get to America. I was just nineteen years old. I didn't speak one word of English. What will life be like for me over there? How would I fit in and adjust to yeshivah life again? I had no problems getting out of the country. I was on my way to America to face a new adventure and new challenges, once again.

The National Bank of Czechoslovakia allowed only $10 in U.S. currency to be taken out of the country by any one individual.

So, "loaded" with those $10 and a few hundred cronas, I took the train from Usti to Prague and changed over to the Intercontinental train for Paris. We passed through Germany and arrived in Paris. There, we had to wait several days before the ship would sail to America. In Paris I met up with two old friends who were also on their way to America: the watchmaker, who was our boarder in Usti, and another man, who was with me in the L'Isle Adam kibbutz and, apparently, also opted out. All three of us were to depart on the same ship. We spent several days in Paris. Luckily, the French banks exchanged my Czech cronas for Franks.

Around the last week in May 1948 we took the train from Paris to the port city of Le Havre on the English Channel and embarked on the *S.S. Washington*, the largest ship (85,000 tons) that I had ever seen, the pride of the U.S. Lines Co. After a few hours, we were on our way, trapped inside a "floating prison," from which there was no way back.

COMING TO AMERICA

The *S.S. Washington* was a huge luxury liner that was partially converted into a troop-carrying vessel. We were put up deep in the lower bowels of the ship, in what seemed to be the dormitory. There were several dozen passengers, all males, sleeping in a large room on bunk beds. They had a kosher kitchen on board. I couldn't eat much. From the second day on till we landed, I was sick to my stomach. We made a stop at the port of Cork in Southern Ireland; otherwise it was nothing but ocean for as far as you could see for the next seven or eight days—a very frightening scene, at least for me.

On June 4, 1948, we docked at New York City, at Pier 22 on the west side. I had just come from a Communist country that had fed us propaganda day and night about the corrupt government of the U.S., how bad the economic situation there really was, and the fallacy of so-called personal freedoms. I, of course, absorbed that propaganda as if it were the actual truth. While we were waiting to be processed by the immigration inspectors, Health Department inspectors, and the HIAS or the Joint functionaries (that took a long time), I went up on the upper deck to inspect this reviled land. When I saw the terrible traffic jam on the west side drive, that was bumper to bumper, I was convinced that all of these cars were ordered by the government to parade in front of the docks to impress the visitors from foreign countries!

Finally my turn came to be processed. When the HIAS people asked me if I had any relatives waiting for me, I said yes, since I did have my cousin waiting for me. This was a big mistake! While all the others, except for those who wound up on Ellis Island, were put up by the HIAS in hotels and were immediately processed as new immigrants and given money for food, transportation, and other needs, I, on the other hand, was told to go with my cousin and report in two weeks time to the Joint office for processing! No money and no accommodations.

Since my cousin was a full-time student in the Mesivta Torah Vodaas and slept in the dormitory with other students, there was no room for me. The yeshivah could not find room for me or for my traveling companion either. They had absorbed many more new students from the survivors' transports than they were able to accommodate. Since we arrived on a Friday afternoon to the Williamsburg section of Brooklyn, where the yeshivah was located, with our heavy luggage, we were put up for Shabbat by some family. On Sunday, we had to find a room somewhere else. My friend and I decided to room together. We finally found a room with an elderly European couple on the Lower East Side, near the Williamsburg Bridge. Our landlords were certain that everything in Europe was just the same as when they had left it some twenty-five to thirty years ago. They proceeded very seriously to introduce us to the modern world. They showed us how to turn on the lights and how to make the water come out of the wall.

There was an electric trolley to cross over the bridge from Delancey Street in Manhattan to Bridge Plaza in Williamsburg. It cost two cents each way. On Shabbat and *yom tov*, we walked in groups across the bridge. It was quite safe to do so in those days. Both sides of the bridge were almost exclusively Jewish neighborhoods. The streets were full with Jewish stores, restaurants, Yiddish movie houses, and stage theaters. Everyone was reading one or more of the four Yiddish daily newspapers. Either the *Morgen Journal*, the *Forwerts*, or *Der Tug*. Even the Communist Party had its own Yiddish daily (I can't recall its name).

After I was settled in my newest home, I reported to the yeshivah. After a long interview, they were convinced that I was a serious candidate for advanced studies. I was assigned to a special class established for people like me. This class was conducted in Yiddish, by a Rabbi Briskman. We did not study any secular subjects or even English as a second language. The entire day was spent studying Talmud and Halachah. Only late at night did I return to my room to sleep.

The $10 that I had brought with me did not last very long. The first two weeks were finally over. I had my first interview with a caseworker at the Joint office, in Yiddish. When she realized my situation, she made my case retroactive to the time of arrival. I was reimbursed for the rent I was paying, and I was allocated a monthly stipend to pay for all of my basic needs as long as I remained a student and did not work for a living. Getting adjusted to life in an uncontrolled free society—where there was no need to carry I.D. papers with you all the time, not to be afraid of the policeman on the beat, being able to buy things without rationing coupons, being allowed to travel in and out of the state and the country—took some time. Especially when you had just arrived from what had become a totally police-controlled, Communist state where every move you made had to be reported and registered.

The last film I saw in Usti just prior to my departure was *Mr. Smith Goes to Washington.* It very powerfully tells the story of the corrupt political system in Washington. Before the film was shown, the political Commissar of Usti came on stage personally and assured us that what we will see in the film correctly and accurately describes the rotten capitalist system of government in the West in general and in the U.S. in particular. He assured us in a very persuasive lecture that "Of course this is one of the ten films that are on the forbidden list to see in the U.S." After seeing the film, he again came on stage to answer questions on the differences between their system of "true democracy" and the corrupt capitalist system. We were all convinced that these were the facts. I couldn't believe my eyes when I saw that this film was being shown in the U.S.! When I asked around to find out if this was just recently removed from the forbidden list, everyone looked at me as if I had just recovered from a dreaded illness. But the power of propaganda had left a confusing set of "truths" in my mind for a long time.

Something happened to me as I fell into the old, familiar, and comfortable routine of being a proper *yeshivah bochur* again. The fact that I again was spending most of my waking hours learning brought with it a strange tranquility and some peace of mind. There was somehow a re-connection with an aspect of the past. My attitude was slowly changing again. I found security in burying my head and mind in the ancient holy books that were once my whole life. I still could not find answers to the very painful questions of why and how G-d could allow such an unspeakable tragedy to befall those who were so close to Him. Neither the *roshei hayeshivah* nor anyone else could give me the answers I so desperately needed. They repeated the "sin" theory, which I could never accept. In the end I had to settle for the "fact" that only G-d alone has the real answers. We will never know. We have to live with that thought, like it or not.

Even though I was now a full-fledged Talmud student again, I was not the same person that I once was when I studied in those Hasidic *yeshivot* in Europe. I had discovered that there were other ways of practicing Torah and *mitzvot* from those that I was trained in as a child. You did not die if you went to the movies or to the beach! The demons and the ghosts were not out to get you. I was living a balanced and sane Torah life, that allowed me to think for myself, read and discover what other cultures were all about. I was now convinced that the great values of the Torah are eternal and that only they could provide me with something enduring and worthwhile to hold on to.

The final boost to my new life was provided, strangely enough, by one of the people who was responsible, in a way, for my rejecting the old ways—the Satmarer Rebbe. He too came to America after he saved his life going to Palestine! My roommate and I were walking by the Satmar Beis Medrish on the corner of Bedford Avenue and Wilson Street on Shabbat morning. I had just a *kippah* on my head rather than a hat. My friend who knew me and my family from home (he, too, had studied in the yeshivah of Chust for many years) argued that I owed it to my father to at least go in and say *"shalom aleichem"* to the Rebbe who was my father's idol. After a great deal of hesitation, we walked in to the *beis medrish*. The Rebbe was in the middle of reading from the Torah. At a pause in the reading, when he sat down to rest a while, we approached him and shook hands with him. (I could no longer bring myself to kiss his hand as I used to do in my previous "incarnation.") He took one look at me and said, *"du bist Dovid theim Teicher's zin"* (you are the son of David from Teich—the name by which my father was known in the "Court" of Satmar). I was completely taken aback! The last time he saw me in Satmar was about six or seven years ago. I was fourteen years old at the time with a black hat and long curly *payes*. I was with my father at the time. Now I was a grown, twenty-year-old man, without a hat or *payes*. How could he recognize me instantly? His *gabbai*, Yosel Ashkenazi, who knew my father well, saw my astonishment. He explained to me later that the Rebbe recognized the Rosenfeld deep-set eyes.

This encounter made me very upset at the Rebbe. If he did recognize me and remembered the closeness that existed between him and my father, why didn't he care enough to inquire about what had happened to him? Why didn't he ask me who of the family had survived? Why didn't he ask to find out what I am doing or offer me his help if I needed it? That proved to me that he wasn't a very caring or sincere person. I no longer had to feel guilty for the way I felt about him personally, nor for rejecting his brand of Yiddishkeit. I became free to pursue and find my own way of a deeply felt love for the modern Orthodox and Zionist way of life that would be based on conviction rather than on fear. I refused to go and see him again, even after I received word that he was asking some of my relatives and even my mother where I was and why I don't come to see him.

Mother had by now crossed the border illegally, at night on foot, with a group of refugees from Czechoslovakia, which was now behind the Iron Curtain, to freedom in Austria. In Vienna, she was placed in a displaced persons camp and she re-applied for an entry visa to the U.S. The quota list for immigration was still very long. Soon after I had left for America Leitchu, too, left for Switzerland. The three of us who had survived now found ourselves once again separated and scattered in three different countries, without the opportunities or the resources to visit each other. I was told that it would be much easier to get mother an entrance visa to Canada, and from there come to the U.S. I promptly got in touch with a lawyer in New York who had experience in these matters so that he might provide mother with an affidavit for a refugee from a D.P. camp to come to work in Canada as domestic help. However, I would have to go to Toronto to obtain such an affidavit or job offer.

I took the train to Toronto, stayed there a few days with a strange family, a wealthy furrier who gave me the needed affidavit. After waiting a few more months in Austria, mother was permitted entry into Canada, which was so much closer to the final destination. She had a very sad experience when she finally reached the shores of the North American continent. She docked at Halifax all alone. There was no friendly welcoming face or voice. She didn't know anyone there, nor did she understand or speak any English. She was also broke. It was in the winter. She was cold and hungry. She passed by a bakery store and went inside to ask for a piece of bread. She didn't have the few cents in local currency to pay for it. They refused to give her the bread!

She cried bitterly on the streets as she wandered aimlessly with her few bundles in her hand. Finally, someone took her to the local Jewish Community office, where they gave her some local money, food, and purchased a train ticket for her to Toronto.

In Toronto she immediately contacted my former Rebbe, the Teicher Rav, who now had a pulpit position there. He had been a very close friend of father. He arranged for mother both a place to stay, with the famous Rabbi Weissmandel family, and also a place to work, as a wig-maker, rather than as a domestic (maid). Life seemed a whole lot better for her now that she was once again able to take care of herself and be productive. However, she never was able to forget the terrible humiliation she suffered in Halifax. She would often remind us of that time in her life.

My health kept on deteriorating. The Joint sent me from one doctor to the next. I was getting uncontrollable and very severe nosebleeds. One time it took a trip to the emergency room of a hospital in New York to stop it. The vitamin and liver injections continued. The constant changes in my life and the need to continuously readjust to new environments, languages, and societies, had not given me an opportunity to work out my deeply felt grief and sense of turmoil and guilt of survival.

I was desperately seeking some meaning for my life and for the "punishment" of surviving hell and being condemned to re-live the past every waking or slumbering moment of my life. Even my talks with some of my *roshei hayeshivah* failed to bring me a modicum of tranquility. They, too, were for the most part, at a loss to understand and to explain G-d's wrath on those of us who were unlucky and got caught in the wrong place at the wrong time.

DECISION TIME

My main problem was still to make an intelligent decision about my future. While I was still a student, I was sent by the yeshivah for the High Holidays to officiate at services at an old age and convalescent home somewhere in Westchester County—White Plains, I think. I stayed there for an entire month from Rosh Hashanah until after Sukkot. This was a great arrangement, since the yeshivah was closed the entire month. I davened for them, blew the shofar, etc. When it came before Yizkor on Yom Kippur, I was supposed to deliver a sermon. Naturally it was in Yiddish, for I still did not know more English than what I had picked up from the street, the movies, and the T.V. It was a total disaster. No sooner did I start to talk about the importance of remembering our loved ones, than I broke down sobbing and getting dizzy to the point that they had to help me off of the pulpit and into my bed. The place had a physician who was also a survivor. He had not had the spirit left in him to start all over again, to study for the Board examinations. He spoke Yiddish. He summoned help from a local doctor who came and left a prescription for some pills.

This incident convinced me that I was not ready either emotionally or professionally to serve as a pulpit rabbi in America. At least not until both my health and my fluency of English improved considerably. I was more confused now than ever before.

Decision time had indeed arrived again. The year of my original student visa had expired. The Immigration Service asked me to honor my pledge to the consulate and return to Czechoslovakia. I did not want to go back there. There was nothing left there for me anymore. The yeshivah got me a lawyer. A lengthy and drawn-out process of hearings and petitions began. The Justice Department refused to grant me a stay. I was called in for hearings almost once a month and interrogated as to why I didn't want to return home. No explanation was accepted. The lawyer even got a New York senator to include my name on a long list of petitioners for a special law permitting those illegal foreigners who for some reason or other could not return to their homes to remain in the States. There were hundreds on that list. The bill passed. Only a handful of names on the list were stricken out from it. Mine was among them! This was not good news. But we kept working on it.

In the meantime, I had moved back to Williamsburg. I had completed my three years of intensive studies at the yeshivah. Alas, my status as an illegal resident prevented the yeshivah Torah Vodaas from officially ordaining me as a rabbi since my student visa had expired and I could no longer be considered a candidate for *smicha*. I was instead sent to see my former rebbe from Europe, the head of the Central Rabbinical Congress of America, an organization of refugee rabbis and heads of European *yeshivot* who granted me *smicha* after both oral and written testing.

I was already so familiar with the Immigration Service that I was sure I could now "wing it" on my own without a lawyer. I registered as a full-time student at the Herzliah Hebrew Teachers Institute, with the aim of becoming a Day School teacher.

After an interview in fluent Hebrew with the Dean, I was allowed to enter as a special student. I was immediately granted two years worth of credit toward the graduation requirements on the basis of my background. I would have to concentrate only on those subjects that I had never studied. I was accepted without a high school diploma.

Our classes were to be taken on Sundays, all day long, and every evening for four hours. I had to find a way to earn a living now. The Joint stopped their stipend as soon as I finished my studies at the yeshivah. My friend, the master watchmaker, found me a job to work with him in a large watchmaking shop. There were about thirty watchmakers there. I was never any good at it. He saw to it that I got to fix only the easy problems, and whenever I could not fix a watch that was assigned to me, he would cover for me and take it home to fix it himself. I now worked at the job on 47th Street forty hours per week and attended Herzliah twenty hours per week. I used to leave the apartment at 7 A.M. to go to the shop, work there till about 5 P.M., grab a quick bite at the school cafeteria (on 91st Street and Riverside Drive), attend classes from 6 to 10 P.M., come "home," eat something, and sit down to do homework.

It was a grueling schedule. I moved out of Williamsburg to a rented room, shared with my friend, on 100th Street, between Riverside Drive and West End Avenue, on the Upper West Side in Manhattan. Later on we moved into a furnished apartment in a rooming house on 83rd Street. We were joined there by a third friend to help out with the rent. He was a graduate of the Hebrew Gymnasium in Ungvar and he also had studied in the yeshivah of Chust. He was very helpful to me with my Hebrew schoolwork, especially with *dikduk*, which was very hard for me to master.

The Immigration Department and I had become an "item." I came up with all kinds of excuses and sad stories of why it was impossible for me to return to Czechoslovakia, a Communist state that persecuted all religions. Nothing helped. The fact that I was no longer a student at the yeshivah, which had sponsored me to begin with, did not make things any easier.

The two years at Herzliah were a tremendous educational experience. A whole new world with wide vistas opened up for me. I became exposed not only to the giants of Hebrew literature and poetry, but also to the great writers and poets of the non-Jewish world. I immediately fell in love with the poetry of Chaim Nachman Bialik. He expressed a great deal of my own feelings.

It was clear to me that his yeshivah background and mine had given us a common point of reference. I understood his pain of "in the city of slaughter" as well as his admiration for the past and for the tradition in *"Mul Aron Hasefarim," "Hamatmid,"* and *"El Ha'agada,"* etc. I found a channel for my own transformation, from the *yeshivah bochur* with the very narrow perspective of several centuries in the past into the more sophisticated and literate being that I felt myself turning into.

The essays of Achad Ha'am, Krochmal, and Luzzatto had given me new insights into the meaning and the philosophy of Judaism. At first I had a very hard time dealing with some of the writings and poetry of some of the more outspokenly anti-religious Hebrew authors.

Through readings and class discussions, I also became familiar with some of the classic thinkers and writers of non-Jewish culture. I learned about Hegel and Schuller. The Indian poet Rabindranath Tagore and his parables became very familiar to me. Nietzsche and Kant and their philosophies captured my interest. Even *Hamlet* I first discovered in a Hebrew translation. The list is endless. Every new name and every new book and anthology brought "enlightenment" in my search for knowledge. The *maskilim* gave identity and legitimacy to my hitherto forbidden thoughts. I relished and enjoyed my newfound "friends." I had entered the twentieth century. Most astonishing of all, to me at least, was the fact that instead of weakening my own deeply held religious convictions that I had rediscovered in the yeshivah, they actually became more firm and more validated by the light of what I had learned and adopted from the fountain of general knowledge and wisdom. I came to look at myself as one of the heirs of the last *maskilim*, the enlightened ones, having learned as much of the original sources of Torah and Talmud as I possibly could before discovering the Enlightenment. There could not have been a more positive route for me to take toward my ultimate destination in life than the path that I was forced to travel. Ever since my graduation from Herzliah, my firm convictions and commitment to Torah and *mitzvot* never again faltered or became remotely subjected to "backsliding." It seems that I may have successfully synthesized and amalgamated the two seemingly contradictory paths into one main road for me to travel on. I learned to think and to act on the basis of both "cultures" without letting the modern overshadow or push aside the basic truths and eternal values of my heritage.

Jewish history was truly fascinating. Flavius, Gretz, Mailer, Yavetz, and Dubnow were hidden treasures, which I discovered and cherished forever. The study of educational psychology has helped me open many new possibilities into understanding my own past and its ambiguities.

Life was never more meaningful to me. However, it seems that all good things have a finite term. Just before graduation, I received two official pieces of paper from Uncle Sam. Both were greetings from the President and from his secretaries. One ordered me to report on a Thursday to Ellis Island for deportation back to Europe, all of my excuses notwithstanding. The second letter ordered me to report to the Camp Kilmer induction center in New Jersey, on Tuesday of the same week! Apparently the Secretary of Defense did not coordinate and disclose his desire to end the Korean "police action" by inducting me into the army, as the ultimate "secret weapon" with the Attorney General's Immigration Service! They should have at least drawn lots between them to see who needed me more urgently.

It may seem silly today, but it certainly was a very serious problem at the time. "What to do now" became once again the ultimate dilemma. If I had reported to Ellis Island and was deported from the country, then I would never again be permitted re-entry, even for a short visit (Mother would soon be coming here from Canada!). If, on the other hand, I reported to the army,

I would most likely end up in Korea as cannon fodder. I was again confused and frightened. Reluctantly, I decided to take my chances in uniform and "play soldier."

Before reporting to Camp Kilmer, I was advised by some friends to go and see the people at the Jewish Welfare Board, who were in charge of the chaplaincy services for Jewish servicemen, to see if I could be enrolled in the chaplain's training school of the army. I could not, because I didn't receive official *smicha* before I left Torah Vodaas, and because of my very poor English language skills. But they did promise to provide me with kosher food wherever I would be. This was very important to me, since I had no intention of eating non-kosher food, no matter what the consequences.

THE GOOD SOLDIER—IZZY

The buses from New York pulled into the gates of Camp Kilmer, New Jersey. The first sight of the fenced camp with the guard towers all around sent an immediate shudder through my entire body. The resemblance to Birkenau was shocking. Although I was quite sure where I was, I could not help myself but to draw an emotional comparison. I broke out in a cold sweat and my heart began racing out of control with apprehension and anxiety. All of my thoughts during the bus trip were intermingled between excitement and adventure and the stark reality that this was wartime and soldiers do get sent to the front and some never come back; others come back wounded and maimed. I kept thinking that I have no one to send me packages from home or come to visit. I would become lost and devoured by the army. I wondered if I had packed up everything that I possessed in the fairly small suitcase that I brought along with me and where I would keep those clothes while playing soldier. I gave up my rented room and quit my job. There was no looking back now. I was going to be a soldier. I was greatly concerned by the fact that my command of the English language was barely passable, for I had decided to be the best soldier that I could possibly be. I was also concerned about the food problem.

When the busses stopped on the parade grounds at Camp Kilmer, we were met by a cadre of drill sergeants and their assistants. We were a sorry looking bunch of raw recruits in a variety of civilian attire, from suit and tie (me) to scantily dressed fellows in sleeveless t-shirts and cut-off jeans. Some were skinny weaklings, like me, while others were brawny and husky, tattooed and pony-tailed.

180

The drill team did not waste a minute on niceties or on welcoming greetings. They barked out orders in a language I had never heard before. I could barely make out some isolated words. I just looked quickly from side to side to see what the others were doing and I mimicked their actions. We were lined up in neat rows (some of these fellows had some previous experiences in military disciplines of drill and maneuver from high school R.O.T.C. membership) and marched off, with our baggage left behind, to a supply barrack where our names were called out and checked on a clipboard every time we received an article of clothing or gear, from olive-drab underwear to helmets and M-1 rifles. We were also given green, class-A uniforms for parades and other festive occasions, and camouflage fatigues for everyday. We were also issued sturdy duffel bags to put everything into. After what seemed a long day, we finally reached the last counter, boots and rifles; we had to sign an official-looking receipt for all the supplies we got. We were sternly warned that we would have to pay for every lost, stolen, or damaged item that we received. The duffel bags were extremely heavy. And so were the rifles (about 10 pounds) and the steel helmets. I had great difficulties carrying those loads. An instantaneous flashback to the first sack of cement dumped on my fragile shoulders in Buna not so long ago completely shocked me. We finally made it to our assigned barrack, huffing and puffing. Each one of us was assigned a bunk, an upper or a lower one. The lower ones were actually avoided by "smart" guys. They were too easy to spot by the sergeants and the lieutenant. It was much easier to be sloppy in an upper bunk. I got assigned to a lower bunk, of course. We also got a footlocker each and a combination lock. There was a specific order on what we could keep in those lockers and how. The sergeants would often inspect them to make sure we were complying with the rules. We were also assigned space in a metal closet to hang up our uniforms.

We were now lined up again and marched back to the parade ground to pick up our civilian luggage and marched back to the barrack. We were told to take out from our luggage only our personal grooming gear (everything was called "gear" in the army lingo) and to send back home all the rest. Those of us who had no home to send the things to were grudgingly given some space in a basement storage area.

The barracks were long wooden frame structures, very much like the ones in Auschwitz and Buna. The sergeant and the corporal had a private room at the entrance. The rest of us, fifty to sixty soldiers, were in one large room with rows of bunk beds on each side of the room, with two footlockers by each double bunk and one steel cabinet by the wall between each bunk.

Our indoctrination began with lessons on how to make up a bed tightly enough to have the sergeant bounce a half-dollar coin off of it. We were given haircuts that left nothing to cover the pate. We woke in the mornings to the sound of bugles from the loudspeakers outside, and the sergeants' barkings from the inside. We had thirty minutes to make our beds, shave, and shower, and stand by the outside of the barrack for roll call, while the sergeant went through the barrack to inspect the beds and the closets. If he didn't like the way the beds were made he would mess it up and you had to spend time redoing it while the others were getting ready for personal inspection while standing at attention at the aisles between the two rows of bunks. This inspection included uniforms, boots, grooming, and the area around your bed. This was done by the platoon commander, a second or first lieutenant.

We were in Camp Kilmer only a couple of weeks. We filled out all kinds of long questionnaires and went through interviews and testing, psychological and aptitude tests.

From here, based on all the testing and interviews, you were assigned to a basic training camp, based on your Military Occupation Profile. I passed language tests as a translator in

Hebrew, Czech, and Hungarian languages. I was also classified as a fine tool and precision instrument fixer, based on my watchmaking experience.

The first free time I had, the evening of the first day, I sought out the Jewish chaplain, a lieutenant colonel, to ask him to provide me with some kosher food. To my astonishment, what I received from him was a stern lecture to forget about my yeshivah days and realize that I am allowed by Jewish law to eat the food the army is providing me. "What will you do when you get to Korea?" he asked me sternly. I was very bitter, tired, and hungry. So I answered him back that I didn't come to ask him for a halachic ruling, and that I would deal with Korea when and if I get there. (I found out later that he was a very liberal, Reform rabbi.) All I wanted to know is if he would provide me with the requested kosher food. I told him that the Jewish Welfare Board in New York assured me that there would be no problem with that. If he had a problem with that, I would have to let the J.W.B. know about it. I saluted and left in anger. On the way to the barrack, I was crying my eyes out. I was still hungry. Did I get myself in trouble on the very first day by being disrespectful to an officer? What happened to my decision to be a "good soldier" and to stay out of trouble?

When we were marched to the dining hall for supper, I ate some dry bread and raw vegetables. I went to the serving window and asked for hard-boiled eggs and a container of milk only. That evening, a corporal came looking for me in my barrack. He called my name and when I came over, he identified himself as the chaplain's assistant and handed me a package with all sorts of kosher foods, including dried salami, cheese, etc. I ate and overate. I was famished. That corporal came every evening while I was at Camp Kilmer with a food package from the chaplain. It does pay to speak up for your rights in this "*Goldene Medine*" (Golden Country).After a few days of orientation, the orders were posted in each barrack where each recruit was going for basic training. After all the tests and interviews, I was assigned to go to Fort Eustis, in Virginia, to train with the Transportation Replacement Command.

Since this was in late fall or early winter, this meant that I would be going down South where it would be a little warmer. It also meant having to confront a new chaplain and new food problems to overcome. We all packed our duffel bags, returned the weapons and other field gear, and boarded buses to our various destinations. We headed southward. We passed by Philadelphia and Baltimore. After about seven to eight hours we arrived at a sprawling military camp, Fort Eustis, just outside Newport News, Virginia, on the shores of the Chesapeake Bay, across the bay from the large naval base at Norfolk. This camp was to be my new home for the duration of my military career.

More orientation and more indoctrination. More standing in formation to go from one place to the next. More vaccinations and more "gear." We found out that our battalion commander was Colonel Foot, our company commander was Captain George Fountain, and our platoon sergeant was Staff Sergeant Richter. We were again assigned bunks, footlockers, and metal cabinet space. I quickly realized that I was in the segregated South, ruled by the Jim Crow laws, designed to humiliate and oppress the blacks. Coming from the liberal New York environment, and as a victim of racial oppression, I had a hard time understanding how this could be allowed to occur in a democratic and free country like America. I suppose that in the back of my mind I was afraid that this could also happen to the Jews. Even though the camp itself as well as the entire army was officially, most recently, desegregated by President Truman's order, it was quite evident that it would take a lot more than a fiat and a lot of time before equality among the races would actually work. The army did try to promote blacks to noncom and to commissioned officer ranks; but that status was worthless once they ventured outside the camp gates.

The blacks, officers as well as enlisted men, always had to move to the rear of the public transportation buses, even when the front seats were empty! In the bus and railroad stations, they had to drink water, sit on benches, eat at lunch counters, and use washroom facilities all especially designated by signs as "For Blacks Only." Other facilities, conversely, were designated as "For Whites Only"! This really bothered me very much. Our company commander, Captain Fountain, was black. He was a highly educated and intelligent person. He had to make a speech the first day of our arrival, that whatever our personal attitude toward blacks may be, we must show proper respect to him as an officer, pointing to the double-bars on his shoulders, reassuring his white Southern subordinates that they are saluting the uniform and the rank, not him, personally.

Most soldiers of my platoon, housed in one barrack, were from the South. They were all like me, reluctant draftees. There was a very clear, albeit invisible, social barrier dividing the whites from the blacks in the barrack and in the dining hall. Only in the ranks during training and maneuvers were we all mixed together. Most of these boys from the South, black or white, had never seen a Jew before in their lives. I recall one guy actually looking for my "devil's horns." To my luck, there were about twenty-five Jewish boys from the New York area in our company, some of them in my platoon. They became my friends and protectors. They ran interference for me when some guys laughed at me when I got up every morning before reveille, to put on my *tefilin* (for prayers). The guys who saw me do this heckled and teased me to come and take their blood pressures, too. My protectors stood up to them. Some of these Jewish boys felt it their duty to protect the Holocaust survivor. This was 1950–51; the wounds of the revelations of what happened to us during the war years were still very open and fresh. Many American Jews developed guilty consciences about not helping their troubled brothers in Nazi-occupied Europe.

A KOSHER SOLDIER

There was no Jewish chaplain at Fort Eustis. I survived on dry cereal, bread, and milk. My newfound Jewish buddies gave me, generously, their own cereals and hard-boiled eggs whenever those were available. However, since we had begun our vigorous basic training, long marches with full pack and rifles, running double time and doing calisthenics and push-ups, my body demanded a lot more nourishment. I was tired and hungry.

My greatest problem, however, was not the food. The long marches began to take a toll on my left leg. The varicose veins and the swelling made the marches a very painful experience. Several times I actually had to "fall out" from formation during a long march and had to be sent back to camp by jeep.

I was truly trying very hard to be the "good soldier" Izzy (that's what my buddies nicknamed me). I was very much afraid of becoming labeled a goof-off and a trouble-maker. One fellow from New York did become the target of the drill cadre as a goof-off. They tormented and "crucified" him for always doing the wrong thing. If everyone else "shouldered" their weapons on the right shoulder, he would use his left shoulder. If everyone turned right, he would turn left. His bed and backpack were never done right. His name was always shouted out by the drill corporals. He was always on the ground doing extra push-ups and on extra K.P. duty. I desperately wanted to avoid such a fate.

As hard as I tried to be the good soldier, I was totally frustrated by the fact that I could not understand the orders barked out by the drill cadre. To my ears every order sounded something akin to "right shoulder harho!" "to the left harhhhh!" With tears in my eyes and fear in my heart, I kept watching what the rest were doing and followed suit. Often, it was too late. I would step with the right foot and everyone else was out of step with me. On some of those occasions, if the sergeant was not in a forgiving mood, I found myself doing extra push-ups or extra practice with the rifle and full backpack. For me, K.P. was a cruel and unusual punishment. I almost fainted from the horrible sight and smell of the pots and pans in which pork, ham, and other such foods were cooked or prepared. Scrubbing those greasy utensils was more than what my delicate stomach could tolerate. On those occasions, I would spend more time in the bathroom hunched over than working. After a while the mass sergeant took pity on me and assigned me only to potato peeling.

My problem with food deprivation grew ever more urgent. A visit to the Catholic chaplain, Captain Fisher, did not help at all. He had no supply of kosher food, nor did he know how to procure some. Captain Fountain had instituted what I thought was a very fair and liberal policy. Every Thursday evening, after regular duty hours, he held "open house," when any soldier could walk into his office without asking for permission to do so from the sergeant or the lieutenant and speak frankly with the captain "off the record" and complain about anybody and anything. I resisted the urge to go and see him, but I got too hungry to play coy any longer. I decided to go and see if he could help me. He was very nice to a frightened and hesitant petitioner like me. He asked me to sit and tell him what was on my mind. As soon as I opened my mouth to state my problem, I was choked up with emotion and anxiety. How would I be able to tell him what my problem was with my broken and halting English?

He was very nice and asked me to relax and tell him why I was crying. When I finally relaxed enough to stop my sobbing, I told him that I was hungry. He was shocked. He couldn't understand why I would be hungry. He asked me why I don't go back for second helpings if I was still hungry? When I told him that I "can't" eat the food, he thought that I was having a problem with the quality or taste of the food. He told me "the food in our mess hall is of high quality. I eat the same food every day."

I finally succeeded in making him aware that I wasn't criticizing the food, but that I still couldn't eat it, because it is not kosher. Being a black man from the Deep South, he had never heard of such a label. He asked me what he needs to instruct the mess sergeant to do in order to make the food kosher. I gave him a condensed lesson in kashrut. Ultimately, he wanted to know what he could do for me. I told him that the only request I have is to be permitted to go into the nearest town, Newport News, where I am certain they have a Jewish community that would be able to provide me with kosher food. This was a tough one for him. The rules were clear that during basic training, no recruits may get passes to go to town. We were to be kept busy twenty-four hours of every day: drills, marches, cleaning of rifles, shining boots, washing laundry, etc. He promised to think about it and let me know.

There was only one other boy in the whole battalion who ate only kosher. I can't recall his name now, but he received packages from home with every kind of food. I had no one on the "outside" to supply me with packages. After a few days, I was summoned to the captain's office. He told me that he checked with the base chaplain, and he confirmed the fact that some Jews will eat only food that was prepared under rabbinic supervision. He had decided, therefore, that in order for me to be able to continue safely with the rigors of basic training, he would grant me a pass every week from Saturday afternoon till Sunday afternoon, with the stipulations that my platoon sergeant has no objections, and that I pass the weekly barrack "white glove" inspections by the lieutenant, and that I stay out of trouble while in town. I was delighted at the prospect.

Basic training became harder and more demanding every day. I started to have great difficulties in keeping up with the rest of the troops during long marches. I fell out of line to rest several times but forced myself up to continue. It occurs to me now that perhaps the memories of the horrible forced marches that I was told about right after the war and what had happened to those poor people who could not keep up with the rest really frightened me enough to make the extreme efforts to keep up with these marches in spite of the terrible pain in my left leg.

The screaming of orders, the fact that I could not understand all of them precisely, and that I could not master the art of looping the rifle sling exactly as demonstrated around my right arm and aim with my left eye (since I could hardly see at all with my right eye) all added to my confusion and frustration.

Surprisingly, I did quite well at target shooting, after I failed miserably the first time around. I even received a certificate attesting to my expertise. But it did not do much for my tormented mind. I became ever more frightened, withdrawn, and anxiety ridden.

The first Saturday inspections came out well after we scrubbed the barrack clean as a hospital operating room. The sergeant gave me the coveted pass to go to town, after a lecture of the dangers lurking in town for soldiers in certain districts. He made it clear that since I am still in basic training, I must wear my uniform even when I am off base. I began walking in the direction of the town. I refused, politely, the offer of some nice civilians to give me a lift to town in their cars. It took me about an hour and a half to get to the center of town. I approached a policeman directing traffic and asked him where I could find a synagogue. He gave me directions to a fairly large building not far away. When I entered the *shul*, I found the rabbi giving a *shiur* on Chumash and Rashi to about thirty or thirty-five congregants sitting around a long table. I took a Chumash from the shelf and sat down at the table. After a few minutes I could not help myself from interjecting some commentaries to the text being discussed. Everyone turned to look at this intruder in uniform.

After the *shiur*, the rabbi approached me and with the most welcoming smile shook my hand and asked me who I am and which yeshivah I came from. He invited me to come home with him after the services. He introduced himself to me as Rabbi Adelman. When we came home, Mrs. Adelman also greeted me with open arms. After *havdalah*, Mrs. Adelman, like a good Jewish mother, sat me down to eat. I finished all of the Shabbat leftovers. I even devoured some turkey, which I had never eaten before or since. I was embarrassed in front of the children. After they had a chance to hear my story and problems, I was assured by the rabbi that Sunday morning he would take care of the food problem. In the meantime I should make myself at home and have a good night's sleep in their home.

Rabbi Adelman asked me if I wanted to earn a few extra dollars teaching at his Sunday school, since I told him that I am a recent graduate of Herzliah. I did. The money came in very handy. And I found out for the first time that I really had some talent as a teacher. The rabbi arranged with the local kosher grocery and delicatessen store an unlimited line of credit to enable me to charge every Sunday, before I returned to base, all the food supplies that I would need for the week. From that day on my food problem was solved. Every Friday, the sergeant would call me to the company office to pick up a package from the Adelmans. In it were two small challahs, wine for Kiddush, and a barbecued chicken. The Adelmans had "adopted" me. I was no longer alone in the world around me.

Later on, when a Jewish chaplain, an Orthodox rabbi came to our base (his family was still in Germany, his previous base), I actually had to share my food with him. Rabbi Adelman was very upset with him, since as an officer he received extra pay for food. I didn't mind sharing my food with him, since that gave me a friend, an officer. We had a little stove installed in the back of the chapel where we warmed up our canned kosher foods.

This "friend" turned out to be anything but a true friend in need. One day, without warning, we were given an order to pack up full gear, helmets, backpacks, weapons and all, to go on a ten-day field maneuver bivouac. As we were being loaded into huge trucks, I saw the chaplain coming down the street. With the permission of the sergeant, I ran to him to tell him that I had no food left to take with me to the field and asked him to arrange something for me with the Adelmans. Instead of reassuring me he began to yell at me, aloud, "How dare you approach an officer on the street!" Choked up with anger, I returned to board the truck with anxiety of what I would eat for the next ten days. I was pleasantly surprised the next day, when my sergeant delivered me the usual package from the Adelmans for Shabbat plus extra canned foods and dehydrated salamis for the rest of my stay in the field. I guess that ever since my bouts with total starvation in Auschwitz, food or lack of it became a major obsession with me, until this day. On my weekly visits to town, I also served as the babysitter for the Adelman children and kept my position as a Sunday school teacher. One of the elderly members of the congregation, a widower, allocated a room in his large house as my permanent home away from home. It was there that I learned the games of poker, *chemin-de-fere*, pinnacle, and other card games. Many years after I had left the army, gotten married, and embarked on a career as a Hebrew teacher, Rabbi Adelman's path and my own crossed once again in Denver.

As the basic training regimen progressed to ever more rigorous physical demands and the maneuvers and bivouac became frightening and took on real possibilities of training for a real war, I became ever more anxious and worried. I did not want to die on the battlefields of Korea. The constant shootings and "forced marches" during the day became confused, in my dreams, with the execution squads and the death marches of the past. I found myself getting up feeling ill more and more often. Very frequently, I reported to sick call at the infirmary with vague complaints of fatigue and generally not feeling good. When the company commander found out that I was consistently unable to complete training assignments and that I was reporting to the infirmary too often, he called me in for a chat, on one of his informal open house sessions on Thursday evenings. He wanted to know what was really the matter. I showed him my carved-up left leg from all those surgeries, and told him of my experiences in the concentration camps.

During that time, I continued as best as I could with the routines of basic training. I even received a certificate of graduation from the three-month-long course. For reasons that only experts in army logic could figure out, I was assigned to continue with training as a transportation trainee. Usually that meant training as truck drivers or amphibious "ducks" drivers—neither of which make sense, since I had no driver's license and had only one workable eye! Luckily I was assigned to harbor craft training. This was the most "glamorous" arm of the transportation core. It rivaled navy training in many aspects. After weeks of classroom lectures on rules of the seas and river navigation, Morse code, and ensign signaling, we were taken to the Norfolk Navy base for fire-fighting training on board ships and oil storage tanks.

Finally, we learned steel cable splicing, a very dangerous task. Now came time to learn how to tie up ships to port installations and rigging flags, etc. At last I was assigned to learn driving and maneuvering small landing crafts, the kinds that carry troops from a large vessel to the beach and the front panel drops open to form a bridge for the troops to land.

During this time, I received a letter from my sister in Switzerland that she was coming to America. Since I was her only brother, she wanted to know if I could come to New York to meet her when her ship arrives. I went to see the Red Cross representative, on the Catholic chaplain's recommendation. I received a week-long pass for emergency reasons. I met my sister and found a furnished room for her. She later moved on to Denver.

One of the great benefits of my army service turned out to be a real bonus. President Eisenhower and Congress passed a law that foreign residents serving in the armed forces would automatically become citizens of the U.S. The base's legal officer filed the proper forms and I was on my way to New York once again to be sworn in as a citizen in a huge hall filled with hundreds of men in uniform.

In the meantime, a board of officers was convened (not a Courts martial) to hear my case for separation from the army. I was told that I would be testifying under oath and that I would be cross-examined just like in a trial. I could have an officer assigned to me as a counselor if I so desired. I didn't. At the hearing of the board, the doctors, the company commander, the platoon leader, and the drill sergeant all testified that I was a good soldier and not a goof-off, that I tried very hard to keep up with the demands of army life, but could not succeed because of my wounded leg and because of the horrors of my past. The board unanimously decided, after asking me all kinds of questions about the concentration camps, to give me a "General Discharge Under Honorable Conditions," which is the same as a regular Honorable Discharge and carries with it all the privileges and benefits of a Veteran G.I.

I was given about $200 in cash as my final army pay. After I handed in all the gear and paid for the few small items I could not account for, I took the bus, as a civilian "Korean War Veteran," and headed back to New York. My army career had lasted a little over four months. Looking back, I realized that even though I was sane enough to realize the obvious differences between Fort Eustis and Auschwitz, still the "gross" picture, the Gestalt, was so close as to make it impossible for the subconscious, especially at night, to distinguish between the two situations. The fences, the guard towers, the uniformed people around me, the shootings, the marches, the angry screams of the drill sergeants, the barracks, the constant fear of the higher-ups, the inability to move around freely, the terrifying thought of winding up in Korea, as indeed my former company and friends did after I left—all of these combined to make life as a soldier impossible for me to bear. However, I never regretted having had that experience. I learned more about life in America, and some English vocabulary, that only living in close quarters with "real" Americans could have provided. And, of course, not having to worry anymore about my immigration status was a great relief. However, once again I had to face, squarely, my all-time problem of what to do next. Where do I go from here? What to do with my life for the next fifty to sixty years?

Mother was still in Toronto and Lea was in Denver. I didn't have the funds or the desire to visit them. I had nothing to offer either of them. I was invited to stay with our friends from Chust until I would sort out my options. I stayed with them for a very short while, in Williamsburg, Brooklyn. I moved back with my former roommates in a rooming house apartment on 83rd Street on Manhattan's West Side.

I began to work simultaneously on two problems: first, to secure mother's visa of entry to the U.S., and second, to find a job for myself as a Hebrew teacher. I did not want to go back to my former job as a watchmaker. I was never really good at it in the first place.

An attorney in New York helped me with my task of bringing mother out of Canada, for a good fee that I had to borrow from my friends. Mother finally arrived, and we rented a small, one-bedroom apartment for her on Bedford Avenue in Williamsburg. I stayed in Manhattan. I came to mother for Shabbat and *yom tov* only. She had her brother living across the street. She quickly found a job as a wig-maker and paid up the loans I made to secure her entry visa. Now I had the time to look for a teaching position.

A TEACHER IN AMERICA

Even the idea of me becoming a schoolteacher would have evoked snickering among my friends who knew me from the old country. But here I was, in America of all places, a fully qualified and certified graduate of a teacher's institute, with a B.A. degree, seriously thinking about finding a teaching position. The culture, the language, and the values of the children that I might be assigned to teach were probably several centuries distant from my own experiences in the small *shtetl* of Chust. They were pampered and lived protected lives. Here, I was told, a teacher may face serious charges of assault for hitting an unruly student. How does a teacher deal with discipline problems? How would I be able to communicate with the students and with their parents? I heard that in American schools, especially in the private and parochial ones, where parents pay high tuition fees, the parents, more so than the principal, decide who is a good teacher. If the parents or the children don't like you, you are history!

Of course I had studied educational psychology, methodology, and lesson preparations, but those were all theory. Those were not meant for people with my background. How would I begin to interact with these "spoiled" children that I had seen on T.V. or heard about in class discussions? I had never, *never*, spent a day inside a school building of a regular day school in the U.S. My sum-total of experience was the couple of hours in Newport News as a substitute Sunday school teacher. I had no idea of what to expect and of how I would deal with my lack of practical knowledge of what goes on in a classroom for an entire day. It is too bad that Herzliah did not insist on student-teaching as a requirement

196

for graduation. It was highly recommended. But since I was busy making a living, working forty hours a week and going to school another twenty hours, I had no time left to spend visiting schools. I faked the "School Visit Observation Report" that I filled out and handed in. Now, I wished I had actually spent the time. It might have discouraged me from pursuing that career goal!

But I had no choices left. I had to give it at least my best shot, before deciding that I was not cut out for that profession. True, I had dreamed all my years as a *cheder* boy that someday I would become a teacher like those fine teachers in the public schools that I attended. But that was a dream. This is reality. That was meant for Chust. This is America. Should I even try? Should I perhaps save myself the crushing embarrassment of failure and ridicule? However, I decided to go ahead and give it a try. After all, I was single, and if things didn't work out, I could move in with my mother, at least temporarily until I would decide what else to do next.

The first thing I needed to do was to secure a Hebrew teacher's license. Actually, I needed two separate licenses: one from the New York Board of Jewish Education that would make me eligible to teach in the metropolitan New York day schools. The other one, from the National Board of Licenses, would give me the privilege of teaching in any Hebrew school in the U.S. My diploma from Herzliah was merely a prerequisite to apply for those licenses. I had to take both an oral and a written test for each one separately.

I went to apply for the national license first. I heard that they are easier to pass. The man who interviewed me and administered the written test was a very sympathetic, elderly, and scholarly gentleman. We got to talking and he showed a real, personal interest in my life's story.

At the New York Board of Jewish Education, the test was much harder and more formal. Here, they gave only temporary licenses to beginning teachers, good for a one-year trial period only. During that year they would send out supervisors to observe you in class and evaluate with you the inspector's findings and recommendations. I began to look for a position in the want-ads sections of the Jewish newspapers. Very disappointing. Everyone wanted experienced people only. Catch 22 at its best.

One day I received a phone call from that nice gentleman at the National Board of License. He found a school that was looking for a teacher for the upper elementary classes who could also teach Talmud. He thought that with my yeshivah and Herzliah background, I would be just the right candidate. He had already spoken with the assistant principal about me and gave me his home phone number to call for an appointment at his home in the evening, since the school was out of the city, in Westchester County.

The assistant principal of the Westchester Day School in Mamaroneck was an American-born and educated young man about thirty to thirty-five years old. He was very nice to me at the interview. He immediately realized my trepidations and he did everything he could to be reassuring and kind. He explained to me in flawless Hebrew, of course, that the job is for a full day and it would pay about $2,800 a year as a starting salary. I found out from him that the opening was for a fourth and a ninth grade position. The ninth-graders were the top class in that school. I would have to teach in *Ivrit* only, no English at all in the classroom. I would have to teach all Jewish studies subjects, including Talmud and *dikduk*.

He told me a little about the school and its students. It was a co-educational, though strictly Orthodox institution. It was run by a headmaster who lived on the school grounds. He was a middle-aged bachelor and a mathematician. He came from Europe, with the Mirrer Yeshivah, I think, and received his advanced degree at Cambridge University in England. He was a stickler for punctuality, decorum, and loyalty. He was the overall administrator of the school, while his assistant was completely in charge of the Hebrew Studies Department. The school was truly an "elitist" one. Only the very rich could afford to send their children there. The school had a most enviable reputation as a prep school, yet the Jewish studies were as important and on par with the secular studies. The religious tone of the place was set by the philosophy of Rabbi J. B. Soloveitchik of Boston, where the headmaster had previously served as an administrator at the Maimonides school.

This place was referred to in the trade as the "aristocratic day school," and rightfully so. It was a sprawling campus of about twenty-six acres of prime land sitting on the shores of the Long Island Sound. The grounds were tucked away in an exclusive neighborhood with a high stone fence around it with a gate and a guardhouse leading into it from the outside. The grounds keepers lived in the gatehouse. The area inside the compound was full of greenery and shrubs of all kinds as well as tall trees. Japanese Bonsai dwarf trees were all over the place, too. There was a baseball field with bleachers and a few tennis courts. (The place also served as a very exclusive summer day camp.)

The main building was actually a mansion, a very large, stone fortress-like building, with lots of rooms inside that now served as classrooms. There was also a music room. The couch-house served as an assembly hall and had a workshop attached to it that served as the arts and crafts classroom. Above it were the headmaster's private rooms. The place used to belong to the Arnold Constable Estate. In short, this school was a few millennia removed from the *cheder* I used to call school in Chust.

The interview went well. In a few days I was notified by the assistant principal to come for an interview with the headmaster at the school. I took the train and got off at Mamaroneck (two stations past New Rochelle). I took a cab to the school on

Orienta Avenue. Once inside the compound I was certain that I would never fit in within a fancy place like this. All my hesitations concerning my choice of becoming a teacher in America bunched up in my throat, and I wanted desperately to escape this "fortress" before I was tossed into the dungeon to be tortured by the kids and their parents like a Marano, by the Inquisitors of Spain. Before I could tell the driver to turn back, we were at the main entrance to the mansion (it had one on every side). A covered and pillared portico led into a very large and empty square-shaped hall. I finally found my way to the office.

Walking through huge, heavy, wooden, engraved doors, I was asked by the receptionist to wait. I was fidgeting in the chair when the assistant principal came out from the "inner sanctum" and took me inside to meet the headmaster. I am sure that he could tell how frightened I was. In his very melodic British accent, he asked me many questions about myself and about what made me think that I would make a good teacher. He threw at me a lot of hypothetical questions about how I would handle certain situations that might come up. He asked me to lay out for him what a typical day would look like in my estimation. He wanted to know how I would divide the available time to cover all the subjects, etc. I had no way of knowing how I did on that interview.

A few days later the assistant principal called me to let me know that I was the successful candidate and that I should meet with him sometime soon to go over the curriculum and school policy guide as well as the daily routines. I was both delighted and worried. After I met with the assistant and signed a one-year agreement, he gave me a written Hebrew curriculum and showed me precisely how he wanted the weekly plan book to look.

It was the summer, and I had ample time to begin preparing for my two grades. I began to think about methods of how to explain complex materials to young students. I came up with ideas for graphs and charts, vocabulary outlines, breaking down issues to their basic elements, etc. Several times I took the train out to the school to become more familiar with the place. The only drawback was the distance. How would I get there and back? It took me about two hours each way and it cost a fortune. I didn't have a car or a driver's license.

I had to take the subway to Grand Central Station or to the 125th Street stop to catch the New Haven train to Mamaroneck and then take a taxi ride to the school. I could not afford the expense. The assistant principal arranged for me to meet another teacher (who later became a close friend), at a subway station in North Bronx, and share a car ride with him and two other teachers. We shared the cost of the gas. Even so, it took me almost two hours to get there and two hours to come back home. But at least it was not so expensive.

Finally, around the end of August 1953, the entire staff began to meet regularly to discuss all the rules and regulations, dos and don'ts, the paper work, the various reports, assembly program assignments, various schedules, lunch and recess duties, discipline problems, outings and field trips, fire drills, and care of books and supplies, etc. It became ever more clear to me that I was committed to become a staff member of a highly prestigious school with lots of pitfalls for a novice outsider who was not at all certain that he actually belonged there in the first place. After the general staff meetings, we split up into two separate sections. The Hebrew staff met with the assistant and the general studies staff met with the headmaster. The curriculum and teaching methods were discussed thoroughly and in great detail.

With trepidation and hesitation, shaking knees and sweaty palms, I showed up for the first day of classes. A last-minute pep talk from the headmaster didn't do much to steady my racing heart palpitations and churning stomach. My classrooms were on the third floor. I had time to observe the onslaught of noisy and excited students. It was too late to back out now. I was totally committed to the position and I had better pull myself together or I would keel over and faint in front of my kids. With a deep intake of air, I managed to greet the students with a smile at the door, as they entered the classroom. We looked each other over carefully. I had to decorate the rooms with posters and pictures, to make them pleasant to the eyes and to have a calming effect on the students. I had also prepared a seating chart and put name-tags on the desks.

By the time the first bell rang, everyone found their seats, not necessarily where they preferred, and were eager to hear what this youngster of a teacher had to say. I'll never know from where I had summoned up the courage, but I heard myself saying in calm tones that we will get along just fine as long as we learn to respect each other's roles in the room. We have a job to accomplish and we can do that either in a pleasant and cooperative way or in an unpleasant and harsh atmosphere. Either way, the job will be done. The choice was theirs. I told them a little bit of my background. They were impressed by the fact that I was an army veteran. I even managed to crack some jokes to set a more relaxed mood in the room. I gave them the task to introduce me to baseball, basketball, and football, of which I had no idea. We didn't waste too much time on preliminaries. Books were distributed, supply lists were given out, and the first lesson began.

To my amazement, I discovered that I had a talent of which I was unaware, a very acute sensitivity to be able to pinpoint the slightest movement or voice coming from behind my back! Without turning around from the chalkboard, I could call out the name of the person talking or getting out of his or her seat. The students were totally impressed and were convinced that I actually had a second pair of eyes on the back of my head. I didn't discourage them from that fantasy; it helped me establish total classroom decorum before there was any chance for a ruckus to develop. I made it a point not to punish for small deviations from the rules, after making the "offender" aware that I knew exactly what he or she had done. I also found out that I had the ability to just stand in front of the desk, hands folded and just look sternly at the ones who were slow in getting organized and ready to learn. It worked every time. They quickly settled down. I made it a point never to begin a lesson or speak a word before I had everyone's total attention. And I would never, under any circumstances, argue with a student in front of his or her peers.

Soon I became aware that I had earned a reputation among my students of being a very strict but very fair teacher. The fact that I was the youngest teacher on the staff helped me in gaining the confidence of my students. They came to me with their peer and parent problems. I really liked what I was doing. I sat up for long hours into the nights preparing interesting lessons and strategies to involve the students in the lesson deliveries and developments. There was a real learning atmosphere in my classrooms.

As the compliments from parents, colleagues, and supervisors piled up, my self-confidence became more evident and I was able to relax ever more as the first year went on. When each teacher was called upon to present and explain his or her program at the first back-to-school night, the headmaster was very flattering in his introduction and made it a point to explain to the parents the great advantage to an "*Ivrit B'Ivrit*" school like W.D.S., of having a teacher on staff "whose Hebrew is even stronger than his English." This melted away my shyness to speak in front of the parents with my broken and heavily accented English.

I made it a point to show to the headmaster and to his assistant copies of the stencils and lesson plans that I prepared, for their comment and approval. I actually pleaded with both of them to come and observe me teaching so that I would know how I was doing. They very seldom found the time to do so. Later on, the headmaster confessed to me that he was not in favor of hiring me. He was worried about my lack of experience and about my general background, but that his assistant persuaded him to take a chance on me. He was very happy that he did. We became good friends. He encouraged me to keep copies of every stencil that I prepared for each subject, with an eye toward the possibility of having them published some day, since there was such a paucity of good workbooks in the Judaic studies area. I listened to his advice and indeed quite a few of those stenciled sheets given out to the students are now in print as workbooks and are used in many schools.

The time came for the supervisor-inspector from the Board of Jewish Education to come and observe me teach, to recommend or reject me for a permanent teaching certificate. I prepared a terrific lesson with all the work sheets and review questions. I was very sure that the inspector would be duly impressed. Dr. Alvin Schiff was assigned to come and observe me. The headmaster escorted him into my classroom. He sat down for about two to three minutes, then got up and left the room! I was devastated. What did I do so terribly wrong that caused such a highly respected and seasoned educator to decide that it was a waste of his time to observe me at least for a while as I developed the presentation? I did something on impulse, driven by fear and instinct to "survive." I left my classroom unsupervised, which should never be done, and ran after Dr. Schiff down the hall. When I caught up with him and asked why he left in such a rush without giving me a chance to prove myself, his answer was comforting and encouraging. He said that he watched the students' faces, their attention and interest in what I was doing. Any teacher can prepare a lesson that will impress an observer. But it takes a master teacher to have the full involvement of all the students and maintain proper decorum in the classroom.

Pointing through the open door of my classroom, he said to me, "When I saw this boy, Roger P., sitting in his seat and intently listening to you, I needed no additional proof that you have what it takes to make a good teacher!" This Roger fellow was the typical "spoiled brat" of the super-wealthy Westchester snobs. His father had a seat at the New York Stock Exchange. His parents were seldom home. They were busy with all kinds of social obligations and worldwide trips. Roger spent the previous summer in a boarding camp where Dr. Schiff was in charge. Roger knew that his father's money would keep him in the camp no matter what he did. So he found all kinds of ways to create havoc and mischief. He even tossed a burning match into the gas tank of a nearby farmer's tractor, which exploded instantaneously and wounded Roger and some of his friends, very lightly. But they could not expel him. Father paid the damages and Roger got to do his "shtick." Dr. Schiff concluded, "When I saw that same Roger sitting and listening, I knew that you had a good way of classroom management and holding their interest. To me that is more important than a planned performance. Don't worry, you passed the inspection. I will recommend you for a permanent license." So he did. In later years when Dr. Schiff became the famous director of the Board of Jewish Education, and we would meet at principals' conventions, we would inevitably come around to wonder what ever happened to "poor-rich" Roger.

We, the faculty members, were always fascinated, at the monthly P.T.A. evening meetings, to watch the chauffeur-driven limousines line up in front of the building and the ladies come out with their mink coats. We most certainly had to pull our punches when discussing their children. Yet, to my great amazement, we did learn a great deal of *limudei kodesh* (Hebrew studies) at a very high level in all subjects. I really enjoyed what I was doing. I was still somewhat unsure of myself, but my colleague and friend was most generous with his time and suggestions. I found myself "hunting down" both the headmaster and his assistant, pleading with them for pointers. I was very serious about becoming a good teacher.

So my first year as a Hebrew teacher in one of the most prestigious day schools in America was coming to a close. I now had a profession that I liked and that I was good at it, too. The graduation ceremonies, the very first ones I had ever attended, were very impressive. They were held on the great lawn, facing the Long Island Sound, on a late Sunday afternoon.

When the school year was officially over, the entire staff and their spouses were the guests of the school's president and his wife, at a barbecue steak dinner on the lawn of their sprawling estate. White-gloved waiters served thick steaks and good wine. Dessert was served with what we thought were solid gold spoons and forks! I told myself, with a satisfactory smile on my face, I have made it in American high society. I was no longer a "greener."

LOVE AT FIRST SIGHT

For most people, I assume, it is not very difficult to decide what to do with a ten-week paid vacation. The beach, reading, taking some courses, going to the movies, the theater, the museums, etc., are probably some popular choices. But for me, like everything else in my life, it presented a real problem and choices to be made. Mother felt that I should learn to drive and buy a car. I was petrified of the idea of driving in New York. I would certainly not pass a driver's test, because of my non-functioning right eye, to begin with. Secondly, where would I get the money to buy a car? And, even if I did get a license and a car, I would never find my way around in New York. I could actually see myself driving around in circles for an eternity, along the various highways, and never find an exit that would take me to my destination. Therefore, I decided not to take mother's advice.

Having worked so hard all year I decided that I needed and deserved a vacation, away from everyone and everything. I decided to go to Israel for a visit of about six weeks. I borrowed some money from my friends and purchased a ticket to Israel.

At that time, 1954, the tragedy of the El-Al plane that was shot out of the skies over Bulgaria, killing all of its passengers, was still very fresh in everyone's mind. It was no wonder that I had butterflies churning in my stomach as I walked up to the huge Boeing Constellation, with the proud display of the Star of David and the Hebrew writings on it. We were on our way. This was another big step forward in my transition from the erstwhile little mountain boy who had seen only one or two automobiles in his first fifteen years of life (until my visit to Budapest).

We flew north (I found out later) to Canada. Our first landing was in Goose Bay, Labrador. It was terribly cold there in the middle of the summer. I think that it was also an American Air Force base at the time. From there we flew to Iceland or Greenland or both. Our next stop was Shanon, Ireland. Next we landed in London. From there we went to Paris, Rome, Vienna, Athens, and Lydda. I became a veritable globetrotter, a man of the big world. Taking a bus to Tel Aviv, transferring to a *sherut* (shared ride) taxi to Kfar Saba, I finally made it to my ultimate destination, my cousin, the Shakets' address.

Kfar Saba was at that time a small town not far from Tel Aviv and near the beautiful city of Netanya with its fine beaches. The Shakets, Esti and Armin, lived a modest little house with their two children. It had been a long time since we saw each other. Esti was genuinely happy to see me and let me stay with them even though the space was quite sparse.

Most of my time I spent in Tel Aviv and on sightseeing buses that took me all over tiny Israel. I spent many days with my other relatives in Israel. Some of my childhood friends from Chust were also delighted to spend time with me. One of my friends from Usti was now a big-shot customs officer in the port of Haifa. He was the head of the unit that inspected all foreign and domestic ships before they could either enter or leave the port. He showed me around Haifa and took me home for a couple of days.

My close childhood friend from Chust, with whom I went to *cheder* and who was my roommate in Teich, was now an army captain in command of a company in Tel Hashomer. He took me around the base and all over Tel-Aviv. He was still single, but he lived with his older brother, and his family when he was off base. He was a career officer and eventually retired as a lieutenant colonel. I also spent some time with my mother's first cousin from Sekernitze, who was now a captain or a major in the National Police, stationed in Tel Aviv. He retired from the Police

Force with the rank of chief inspector. Eventually he moved to Argentina. I was not bored.

The remainder of my time, when I was not traveling around, I spent with my cousin and her two small children, or at the beautiful beach in Netanya. Even though I never learned how to swim, I still enjoyed going to the beach. I stood with my back to incoming wave after wave of pure blue-green water, jumping up with each wave. I was content to lull in the sun on a beach lounge. However, my cousin Esti was not one to just let her guest enjoy himself quietly. She decided to go on a crusade. She decided that it was high time for me, at the old age of twenty-six, to find a nice Israeli girl, get married, and settle down in Israel.

Time was now running short. It was mid-August and soon I would have to report to W.D.S. for planning sessions, before the school year commenced. I began to get ready for the return trip home. As I was gathering the souvenirs and gifts that I had bought to take home and find a place for them in my one suitcase, I discovered, to my astonishment, that I had completely forgotten to deliver Selma's (she was my sister's roommate and close friend in Denver) package to her sister in Tel Aviv! Quickly, I wrote her a postcard, in Hebrew, of course, telling her that I was too busy to deliver the parcel in person, since I was not planning to be in Tel Aviv before I left, on the nearest Sunday. If she wanted to come and pick it up, she could come to the Shakets' home in Kfar Saba to do so. If I was not there, I would leave the package with the family there. There was no telephone where I could get in touch with her. I sent the postcard and forgot to be concerned about it any longer. It was up to her now.

The last Friday of my visit arrived. Sunday I would be on my way back to New York. I decided to spend one more day, or part of it, at the beach in Netanya, this time by myself. I took my camera, my tourist's tote bag, put on my shorts, and was off to the beach. Toward the middle of the afternoon, I took the bus back to Kfar Saba, sad that the first real vacation was all but over.

As I started to walk away from the bus station, deep in thought, I heard what sounded like a lady's voice calling me. I turned around and saw a most beautiful girl pursuing me. She introduced herself as Tova Lock, Selma's sister. She had already been at the Shakets' and retrieved the package. I asked her if she had time to have a cup of coffee with me in a nearby kiosk. We sat down at a table to enjoy our coffee and cake. We seemed to enjoy each other's company much more than the food and drink. We could not believe how many things we had in common, besides the fact that our two sisters were best friends. (Later, I found out that this was all a plot cooked up by our two sisters in Denver to bring us together. It worked.) We were both survivors. We both spoke Hebrew and Hungarian. We both had lost our fathers in the Holocaust. We started talking about our backgrounds and traditions from home. We really had a very similar outlook on what was important. We were quoting whole passages from Tanach (Bible) to impress each other.

I was curious to know why she stuck around in Kfar Saba on a Friday afternoon after she got what she came for? She told me it was curiosity, to meet me after my cousin, Esti, described me to her, and her little Shoshi, age about five or six, asked her if she was going to marry her "uncle" from America. After a while we had to say our goodbyes. It was getting late and she still had to catch a bus back to Tel Aviv before Shabbat. I was badly smitten with that girl. I could not get her out of my mind. She was so beautiful and so intelligent. All day Shabbat I kept admonishing myself for not getting to know her earlier and to be able to spend some time with her.

For the first time in my life I began seriously to consider marriage and settling down to raise a family. I was now at the same age as my father was when he got married. Not that this was of any importance at all; it was just another push in the right direction.

I reached a decision. I would postpone my return trip to New York and spend some time with her. The first thing Sunday morning, I took a bus to the El-Al office in Tel Aviv to postpone my return trip by about ten days. I then sent a telegram to the school, notifying them that I would have to miss the first few days of conferences. Then I sent another telegram to one of my close friends, to cable me some money, via Western Union. I was broke. He did send me, immediately, $50, a lot of money at that time. I sent Esti to go to Tova's place of employment, to let her know that I extended my stay because I wanted to see her again, and that I will wait for her after work.

We met again. Apparently, there is such a thing as love at first sight, after all. But the fact that we were both convinced that we were right for each other after just one short meeting, and that I was willing to risk my job, and she, to alter her future plans, all on account of our brief encounter, that is still a very rare kind of love! We had found it.

We went out to dinner and to the movies. I met her mother, who was also quite happy about the turn of events. Tova's brother and uncles were very satisfied and completely impressed with my yeshivah background and by the fact that I was teaching Talmud and other sacred materials. We saw each other every day. We talked a lot about everything and especially about life in America. As I got to meet the rest of Tova's family, I became impressed with her *yichus*, too. Her mother's brothers, and brother-in-law were all *talmidei chachamim* (scholars) and rabbis.

There was one curious, almost amusing detail, that kept buzzing in the back of my mind. Her entire family, and Tova herself, were Oberlanders, born and raised in Vienna and in Presburg, the cradle of Jewish high culture. Tova was raised on operas and on classical music. I, on the other hand, was an Unterlander, which was the extreme opposite of the Oberlander. We were of Hasidic upbringing and they were of Ashkenazic and Mitnagdic (anti-Hasidic) background. Before the war, such families seldom, if ever, intermarried. We were considered uncultured peasants and they were the aristocrats. We spoke Yiddish and they spoke *Hoch Deutch* (German). They went to shows and to concerts, and we went to the Rebbe. They were "civilized" and we were "primitive." Later on we often wondered whether anything could have ever developed between us romantically, if things would have remained as they were before the Holocaust. Would our parents ever have agreed to such a "mixed" marriage? Probably yes, but very reluctantly. The Holocaust was the ultimate equalizer of the remnants of our people.

We decided to get married. On the following Thursday we had an engagement party at the home of Tova's aunt and uncle in Tel Aviv. Many of my friends from Chust came to help us celebrate the happy event, in addition to our family members. There was no time left for a wedding. We sent a telegram to let mother know and she informed our sisters in Denver. (Those two conspirators and puppeteers had pulled the strings by remote control all the way to Israel, and the two of us willingly performed according to their script!). We made plans for me to come back to Israel in December, during my winter break from school, and get married then. In the meantime, Tova was to start working on her legal papers, passport, visa, military release, *sochnut*, etc.

I had to return to work, ever so reluctantly. I began making plans to prepare for our future lives together. I went apartment hunting. I bought a new suit at Ripley's on Delancey Street, which I paid up in $5 monthly installments. I started saving every penny I could. Mother, as usual, was there to help whenever we needed her. She gave me the $400 to buy Tova an engagement ring and a wedding band. Looking back, I realize how tough it must have been for mother to see her only surviving son making plans to marry a girl that she had never seen, or knew anything about. How would Tova and I have felt if our sons would have done so? But, I was out to prove to myself, that I was independent and could do as I pleased, without taking mother's feelings into account. But there was no way for the two of them to meet. Neither of them had the means to travel to meet the other.

Time seemed to crawl very slowly. I was very anxious to return to Israel and marry my dream girl. We corresponded in Hebrew and in Hungarian. We were both counting the days, full with hope and excitement of what the future will hold for us. My friends were very discouraging. We had all heard stories of Israeli girls marrying American tourists just for the purpose of coming to America, and then abandoned their husbands and even extorted money to agree to a *get* (Jewish divorce decree). I was convinced that my heart was not misleading me.

We were married on the 16th of December 1954. I returned to New York about the 10th of January 1955. It took Erica (or Tova) about two more months to get everything in order to enable her to come home to me. Finally, I again borrowed enough new money to buy Erica a one way plane ticket on KLM. I moved into our new home and began to make it ready for Erica's arrival. She arrived in New York around the beginning of March. I filled up the refrigerator with all kinds of goodies. The day of her arrival, I took off from work. Erica had sent me a telegram with the flight number and time of arrival. I was terribly excited. I left for the airport at least four hours before the plane was due to arrive. I could not stay home any longer. When I arrived at the KLM counter to find out if the flight would arrive on time, I was told that this flight had landed a few hours ago! Obviously, there was some mix-up somewhere. I was devastated for I could not find Erica anywhere. Finally I found her at the El-Al ticket counter. She was ready to take a flight back home, convinced that I had a change of heart. Nothing could have been further from the truth!

The first Shabbat together we spent at my mother's home in Williamsburg. To my great relief, Erica and mother got along very nicely. Mother was impressed, when she saw Erica take a *siddur* and began to daven the Friday night prayers, while I went to *shul*. Erica liked Williamsburg very much. It was teeming with Hungarian, Yiddish and Hebrew speaking young people. From the window we could watch all the young boys and girls "parading" on Bedford Avenue. The street was alive with chatter and laughter. People would stop by at the window to chat with mother and be introduced to her daughter-in-law. Erica wanted very much that we should move to Williamsburg. I would not hear of it.

Our first son, David was born on April 16, 1956. He suffered from asthma. The damp New York climate was not very good for him.

We heard from the doctor and from others that the dampness of the New York air was definitely not helping David. Some people advised us to move to Arizona. Others felt that Colorado might be the right location to at least ease the severity of his attacks. Of course, we did not have the means to pick up and move thousands of miles away, without the certainty that it would make a difference in David's condition. And what about finding a job, wherever we would move? This went on until the summer of 1958, when David became two years old. We were desperate to find a way out of our miseries.

It seems that when you think that everything goes against you and that you are doomed and trapped in your circumstances, G-d prepares a way out for you.

One of my former colleagues from Westchester Day School came through for us. We had become very friendly. He was older than I and he was a graduate of Yeshiva University and held a master's degree in education.

In 1957 he became the principal of Hillel Academy Day School in Denver, Colorado. He appreciated my competence as a good educator, with five years of very successful teaching experience. In the spring of 1958 he needed a Hebrew speaking teacher for the upper grades (6th through 8th) of that school. He offered me that position, with a raise in salary and a lower cost of living in Denver than in New York. Since he knew me and he vouched for my proficiency, I didn't even have to come out for an interview. This was a godsend opportunity to take David to a drier climate.

We decided that even though we would be leaving behind my mother, and leaving a secure position, it was worth the try. It also meant that Erica would be near her sister, Selma, who also lived in Denver. I accepted the position. The headmaster at Westchester Day School assured me that a job would always be available for me if things didn't work out well in Denver. I signed a one-year contract with Hillel Academy of Denver.

Moving to Denver

With the headmaster's assurance that I could always come back, it was much less traumatic to say our goodbyes to my fellow teachers, family, and friends. We did not burn our bridges, we assured ourselves. We could always come back to W.D.S. We began the very easy task of packing up our very meager belongings. A couple of old suitcases took care of all of our tangibles. The furniture (a very expensive bedroom set), our few dishes, the T.V. set and my books, we sent away by a moving truck.

We purchased train tickets and we were on our way once again, to start live anew without knowing what lay ahead of us in that far away town. Traveling almost 2,000 miles away from our fragile home base was very hard on our nerves. We had no idea what to expect nor where we would put down our head once we arrived in that distant "frontier" town that was so familiar to us from all those Western movies we were watching.

The secretary of the school picked us up from the train station. Somebody, I don't recall who, rented for us a dingy basement apartment, with very few pieces of furniture in it, on the corner of West Colfax Avenue and Osceola Street on the west side of town, the Denver Jewish ghetto. The basement was dark and very depressing. We went out to buy some food. Soon we realized that without a car you are very limited in your ability to get around.

We were very depressed. We missed New York very much, and especially the people we left behind. Of course I missed mother and felt somewhat guilty for depriving her once again of her rights as a mother and a grandmother.

Finally, we began to look for a decent apartment and to begin learning to drive, to give us independence. After two weeks in the basement, we found an apartment on Xavier Street. It was a very nice and comfortable place.

Almost miraculously, David never had another asthma attack since we arrived in Denver. The air at that time was still one of the cleanest in the country. That, in itself, made the move more than worthwhile.

However, we still missed New York, with its teeming and bustling Jewish life. We felt isolated in Denver. During the summer, I took driving lessons and passed on my first try. We were elated. We bought a used 1953 Chevrolet, the kind that still had a split windshield. To us, it was the most beautiful machine in the world. We paid $350 for it. I began to learn how to get around in town. One thing I never mastered was driving on the highways and in the mountains.

When I began teaching the oldest grades, I found that children were not different from one city to the other. You treat them fairly and challenge them mentally; they will respect and even get to like you.

In a relatively short time we made some friends in Denver. Life was really good. I became a very popular teacher with both the parents and with the students.

About two years after moving to Denver, our family grew to four. Our second baby was on its way to join us.

On Shabbat Chol Hamoed Pesach, 1960, at about 9 or 10 A.M. our second son, Meir, arrived at St. Anthony's Hospital in Denver.

TEACHER—AUTHOR—PRINCIPAL

Our lives in Denver continued to be pretty good. We finally bought our own first home on 1415 Yates Street. I continued to be a popular teacher with the students, colleagues, parents, principal and with the Education Committee of the school. We enjoyed living in our own home, which was just large enough for our needs. It was a small house with a very large back porch and an enormous backyard, with a built-in playhouse. The children enjoyed the friendship of the neighborhood children and the comfortable outdoor play areas.

As the years of my tenure as a teacher of the upper elementary grades went on, I had accumulated a large storehouse of "ditto" stencil sheets and notes of all the different lessons in all subjects which I was teaching. I developed new approaches and materials for my classes. I had become somewhat of an expert on preparing written materials as aids in the teaching of all the Hebrew subjects: Chumash, Rashi, Gemara, History, Navi, and *dikduk*.

I was particularly proud of my handwritten materials in the form of duplicated sheets to serve as worksheets and vocabulary study guides in the beginners' Gemara (Talmud) classes (grade 6). I decided to put those together as a workbook. I gave them to my principal, to take a copy of the workbook with him to the principal's convention of Torah Umesorah, the umbrella organization of most American and Canadian Day Schools. He brought me back very encouraging evaluations from many principals who read the volume.

Tova encouraged me to sit down and prepare a "camera-ready" version of that volume and try to find a publisher for it. I got very excited about the prospect. It would channel my concentration from focusing on the horrors of the past, to a creative future.

The first step was to acquire a portable Hebrew typewriter, which we did on our next trip to New York. It was a very compact lightweight Hermes. I kept working on the manuscript while teaching a full load. However, with the enthusiasm of my newly discovered talents as a publishable author, I began using my new toy, the Hermes typewriter, to write some articles on it in Hebrew, on a variety of curricular approaches and on the need for focusing on the main goals of day school education, for publication. Two such articles were actually published in the Torah Umesorah, monthly magazine for the educators, *Hamenahel* (The Principal). One day, I was called by the editor of the *Jewish Parent Magazine*, also published by T.U., for the parents' understanding of the educational values and materials of the day school curriculum, to submit an in-depth explanation of the place of the parent in the Gemara program (since most parents did not have a yeshivah background, and could not be of assistance to their children who were apprehensive when this new and highly intellectual material was introduced to them in the fifth or sixth grade class).

This magazine was in English. When this lengthy article was published and was well received by both the parents and the educators, I was finally convinced that this was for real. I was an *author*! The little mountain boy from the "uncivilized old country," with a barely sixth-grade general education and a survivor of the worst hell on earth, had something to contribute to the civilized field of modern education and educational psychology? Heady stuff, indeed!

Now, I began to type my "magnum opus," the workbook for beginning Talmud students with exercises and graphics, vocabulary lists and tests, geared to make this complex and mysterious subject user-friendly. I worked diligently, day and night, all summer long, typing away with two fingers. (To this day I have not managed to learn how to use a typewriter or computer keyboard in a more proficient manner.) It took me about three months of typing, erasing, changing, editing, etc. Finally, I had a completed workbook with as few errors in it as I could manage. It looked pretty impressive. It contained 134 pages.

I asked an attorney friend of mine to get me a copyright registration for it. He did. I called it *Gemara L'Matchilim* (Talmud for Beginners). It contained twenty-three lessons (or chapters) with introductions, exercises, reviews, tests, and halachic decisions. It was based on the actual lessons that I taught for the past ten to eleven years, on the fourth chapter of *B'rachot*.

Now began the search for a publisher and distributor. I spent the winter break from school to fly to New York with my manuscript. I went around with it from one publisher to the other—no takers. I even offered it for free to Torah Umesorah Publications. They argued that: 1) There were not enough schools that have this particular tractate in their curriculum to make it a good investment, and 2) It was "too revolutionary" a concept to teach Talmud with a sound, new, and modern method. I came back very disappointed. I was still convinced, from my empirical experience, that my approach was sound. I also had a well known *posek* in New York look over my halachic conclusions, and he had agreed that they were accurate.

I was absolutely convinced that if other educators would see this work and its great value in helping the students overcome their fears of this subject, they would readily adopt this material into their curriculum. My problem was how to go about finding a publisher who would share my convictions and enthusiasm for this project and would be willing to take a chance on someone unknown in the field with a different approach. Since I could not find such a publisher, my wife and I decided that we must find the funds necessary to publish it ourselves, and then try to sell the copies ourselves from our home.

We went to see a printer that we knew in Lakewood, Colorado. In the meantime, I had decided to write and type out a companion volume for the teacher which contained detailed plans, suggestions on how to introduce each lesson, related materials, and the answers to all of the exercises and tests. Since this volume would have very limited circulation, I decided to mimeograph the fifty or so pages. I needed the printer to make the covers and binding only for this volume. After many days of negotiating, he finally agreed to a special fee of $2,000 for 1,000 photo-offset, bound copies. That seemed like a fair deal. I was convinced that I would be able to sell them for at least $4.00 each.

Alas, we did not have the needed $2,000! I decided to swallow my pride and went to see a certain wealthy supporter of Torah institutions, and borrowed the money from him. In return, he asked me to write in a dedication in memory of his late mother-in-law. I agreed to do that. (I did not think of it at the time, but it is clear to me now that this was against Halachah since it constituted a form of interest on the loan.)

For several weeks I spent most of my time at the printer's shop, correcting and changing as was needed. Finally, I took possession of the books and took them home. I bought myself a bookkeeper's ledger, as well as a receipt pad. I stored the books in our home and they took up a large part of our small den. I consulted the Torah Umesorah Register of schools and picked out about forty or forty-five schools that were large enough and modern enough to be interested in this work. I sent a free perusal copy to each of the principals of those schools, with a letter detailing the benefits of this work. By this time, the school year 1965–66 had already started. I was worried that I would have to wait another full year before anyone would put in an order.

I was wrong. About two to three weeks later, my wife called me at school, all excited. The first order for 100 copies had just arrived from a school in New Jersey. The order was accompanied by a check in full payment and a very gracious letter praising my new approach and methodical structure of the workbook. We were elated. The orders kept coming in almost daily. I sold out the entire stock by the end of the winter. I paid back the loan in full and even had some profit left over for us.

More orders and reorders kept coming. I did not want to reprint the books. I was satisfied in the knowledge that my work was appreciated and that I had made myself a name as an expert in curricular matters. All inquiries were referred to the publications department of T.U., who was in the business of publishing and selling educational materials. I did not have to wait too long. The director of publications called to tell me that he wanted to republish these two volumes. This time, we agreed that I would not offer it to them for free. I would be getting annual royalties at fifteen percent, the same as all other authors. These workbooks became the most popular item in the T.U. catalog. (It was reprinted twenty times by now.) I still receive my annual royalty checks of $2–3,000 dollars.

I was still teaching my classes at Hillel. Now, Torah Umesorah asked me for more workbooks on any subjects that follow the same approach. I sat down once more to edit and prepare for publication two volumes on the book of *Bamidbar* (Numbers) with Rashi's commentary. I bought a larger typewriter to type out the manuscripts and sent them to T.U. They were immediately published. They, too, became a staple item in the day school curriculum. They too have been reprinted at least a dozen times. I still collect annual royalty checks for those two volumes, also. All together T.U. published nine of my books.

My name became known in day school circles as a competent educator. I continued to submit articles for publication in the *Hamenahel* as well as other professional journals.

When we first came to Denver in 1958, the school had just been five years old. It had no building of its own. Classes met in various synagogue classrooms. In the summer of 1958, an old abandoned, pink public school building was purchased for Hillel. Everyone was excited. Work parties of parents, students and other interested people came to the building to help spruce it up after the long years that it stood unoccupied. Some were painting inside and out. Others were scrubbing the floors and the windows or pulling out the overgrown weeds from the front and the back yards. Tova and I participated in the work, willingly. We were caught up in the great excitement.

In 1966, the building became too small to accommodate all of the new students that came flocking to the very reputable day school. A modernistic and spacious new building was put up behind the old pink one. It is a beautiful and large edifice. In the summer of 1966 the building was dedicated with great fanfare. Classes began to meet in the new building. The school choir and band participated in the festivities. Hillel Academy was one of the few Torah Umesorah Day Schools that was daring enough not only to be completely co-educational in both areas of study, secular and sacred, but one that had art, music, a choir, and P.E. programs as well.

The music director was a very fine teacher with a broad background. Under his direction, the students had put on musical performances for the entire community. Such operettas as *The Mikado*, as well as many other Gilbert and Sullivan musicals, performed by a co-educational cast and choir, were not really acceptable to everyone, but all of the students, even those from the most religious homes participated in those performances without anyone ever raising an objection. Those were years of total harmony among the parents and the students. The school's reputation was one with very high standards of academics and with an open, welcoming attitude toward all members of the community, while maintaining a strictly Orthodox profile. Hillel was at that time a strictly *Ivrit b'Ivrit* school. (All Jewish subjects, without any exception, were taught in the Hebrew language as the vehicle of instruction.)

After the first principal, my friend from Westchester Day School, left the school, things started to move to the right, slowly. There were no more mixed choirs, and no more musical performances. The genders were separated for all of the Hebrew studies in grades 7–8 and then recombined into two homogeneous classes; each was combined with both seventh and eighth graders of the same sex, together, one class for boys and one for girls.

Apparently not everyone was happy with this trend. The new principal, too, left Hillel at the close of the 1966–67 school year, after serving only three years. He moved to Israel. We were away from town for most of the month of July 1967. In August, all of the teachers were notified by letter from the chairman of the education committee that a well known, long-time principal of a famous day school, had been engaged as the new principal. His picture and biography were published in the local Jewish news.

About one week later, we were again notified by letter, that the intended principal had reneged on his commitment. (He had breached his contract with the school.) It seems that he used the Denver contract as a lever in his negotiations with his board of directors. It was getting very close to the beginning of the next school year and no new principal was hired. All kinds of rumors were circulating about possible candidates coming and going in and out of town. I was still busy writing articles and preparing materials for the approaching school year.

One evening I received a phone call, out of the blue, from the president of the school board, asking me to come over to discuss an important matter. I told Tova that I had a premonition, a gut feeling, that I would be offered the principal-ship. Tova thought that I was kidding myself. How could a school like this, with a national reputation, even consider to engage an unknown refugee, without a secular college degree (or even a high school diploma), with a minimum of language skills in English, to be the principal? The parents would never go for it, especially now, when the school had just applied to the State Department of Education to become accredited. One of the requirements would be that the principal have a Master's degree in educational administration and a valid Administrators License (Type D) from the State Department of Education! It was truly sheer fantasy on my part.

After considering all possibilities, Tova and I decided that, if perchance, I would be offered the position, I would take it, and work out the problems later. After all, this would mean the highest form of recognition, a promotion and a lot more income to be able to afford some of the material things we never could even dream of having.

When I arrived at the appointed meeting place, I found there the entire education committee, plus some of the former presidents of the school. My knees were shaking and my heart was racing. Dr. Irving Mehler, the chairman of the education committee, asked me that since I am aware of the situation at the school at this point in time, if I would consider myself a serious candidate as principal. My mind began racing. Could it really be? Even though Tova and I had decided that if I was offered the position, I would accept it, suddenly I was not so sure of myself. But, in back of my mind there was a silent voice telling me that this is the great break and my chance to prove to myself what stuff I was really made of. I took a long hard look at the faces in the room. I began to present my answer, slowly and deliberately. To paraphrase the essence of my presentation would sound like this: "As I look around here, there isn't one person here whose children were not in my class for at least a couple of years. I have been a classroom teacher for fourteen years, nine years here and five years at Westchester Day School. You all know, and I know, too, that I am an effective educator. You have never had any reason to doubt that fact, so you can be sure that if I take the position, I will make certain that the educational standards of the school will be maintained and even improved. I know the community well and I know the 'hierarchy' order of the school boards, committees and their personalities. It would take any outsider, coming into the community, several years to find that out. I am intimately familiar with the inner workings and schedules of the school. I know the strengths and the weaknesses of the curriculum, of the teachers and of the support staff. You know that my philosophy and outlook are those of a religious Zionist. "I know that I am a good teacher, but neither I nor you will ever know what kind of an administrator I'll be unless both you and I are willing to give it a try. I will promise you to try my very best to earn your trust. I have only one request—since my English is not perfect, I don't want to be put in embarrassing positions of being asked to make public speeches. I do not want more than a one-year trial period. If it works out, fine; but if not, I'd be very happy to return to my classrooms as a full-time teacher. And, since we are both taking a chance on each other, and the fact is that you don't have much time left before the school year begins, and that you will have to find, at least temporarily, a person with credentials in the secular realm, until I have the opportunity to acquire the needed university credits to satisfy the authorities, I'll make you an offer that will make your decision easier. For this coming year, I'll teach a half day and do the administration duties the other half, as well as during all of the free time I'll be able to find." I very strongly hinted that since this will be a novel experience for me, the board and its committees allow me to work out any problem that might come up, my own way, without them looking over my shoulder or their interference.

We then discussed the conditions of employment that the school would offer me, i.e., salary, convention travel, vacation, insurance, etc. The rest of the evening was spent in questions and answers on some specific ideas I might have on improving the curricular and especially the co-curricular and extra-curricular programs of the school.

I left the meeting with a very relaxed feeling of confidence. The school president called the next morning telling me how absolutely impressed the group was with my presentation and with my confidence to be able to handle the duties of principal. The group unanimously voted to offer me the position, giving me a free hand to begin work on all necessary matters and spend the necessary funds needed to make sure of a smooth opening day. He asked me to stop by his office to pick up the keys to the building and to *my* office. That was it. Little Sruli from the little *shtetle* Chust, the boy who barely survived his teenage years, the little immigrant boy who discovered not just a new continent, but a whole new universe, called "civilization," the one who was still completely consumed by self-doubt and guilt, the one who never finished elementary school, had now become transformed into Rabbi Israel Rosenfeld, principal and administrator of one of the most prestigious American Jewish day schools. This was a "miracle of miracles," indeed! There was, after all, a good reason for my life being spared. Tova and I were overcome with ecstasy. We knew that it would not be easy. How would my colleagues and coworkers accept the fact that I was promoted and would be their direct supervisor and boss? How would the students be able to switch their thinking of me as the principal, when they were used to for so many years seeing me as just another teacher? I would really have to work on these matters.

The first thing I did was to write a letter to the staff, following the official letter they received from the school's president. In it I solicited their input and ideas on how to better serve the educational needs of the students. Then, I called some of the key teachers in both areas of study to assure them that any changes would be made as a group effort and that I would seek their input in all areas. I assured them that as a classroom teacher of fourteen years, I have felt, with them, the same frustrations of being ignored, underpaid, overworked, and underappreciated. I pledged my total efforts to work with them to improve our very low status in all possible matters of mutual concern. Some responded enthusiastically, while others expressed open hostility and defiance.

We looked around for a person to fill the position of Secular Studies Coordinator, to satisfy the Accreditation authorities, as well as those parents and staff members who had qualms about my lack of the proper certifications. I insisted from the start not to create an assistant or co-principal's position for this purpose, since I was convinced that you can't have two separate heads running one institution from two differing viewpoints. Only one person at a time must be fully in charge; only then can he be held accountable for what is going on. Luckily, we found just the right person. Ms. Biddick, a non-Jew, had the best credentials possible. She was a recently retired principal from one of the local Public Elementary schools. She knew the exact requirements of the Accreditation Department, and some of the people running that program. She was also willing to take a position that would be subordinate to an overall principal. She did not have an ego to feed, nor an ambition to embark on a new career. She had a wonderful personality, was friendly and always willing to learn new ideas and differing approaches. She was hired to be the coordinator, on a temporary basis, until I would be able to earn the needed credits to fulfill the requirements.

Ms. Biddick and I worked out an understanding that I would decide on all matters of policy and philosophy of the school. She was of enormous help to me in assuaging the fears that I and others had regarding my lack of qualifications to be the principal of a high standards school such as Hillel Academy.

School opened on time. Everything was functioning well. I had previously held individual meetings with each teacher and discussed their programs and possible updates and changes, in the schedules and materials. Two full days of general staff meetings were held prior to the opening of school to discuss administrative procedures and to answer all questions regarding the dos and don'ts for a smooth transition and for a successful year. I felt that I had succeeded in gaining the loyalties of almost all of the teachers, with the notable exception of one. He was brooding. He told me, outright, that he had better qualifications and credentials than I (he had a master's degree from Harvard University) and that therefore, I should not have accepted the position! I tried very hard to gain his cooperation, but was not very successful.

Immediately after I took over, I instituted some needed changes and improvements. I set aside every last Friday of the month for children to be dismissed at noon, to facilitate general faculty meetings. Half of the afternoon was devoted to discussing upcoming events and critiques of the month past as well as to hear new ideas anyone may have. On the faculty room bulletin board I posted a proposed agenda for the meetings, and teachers were encouraged to suggest additional topics they wanted to have discussed. All of those anonymous suggestions were included in a typed agenda sheet, which was distributed to all faculty members prior to the meetings. The second half of the afternoon was always devoted to an in-depth in-service session with outside experts in various educational aspects. Most of these people were professors teaching in local universities.

Additional, intensive evening in-service programs, which awarded credit points, needed for recertification, as was suggested by the teachers, were also set up and paid for by the school. A Parents' Handbook, containing school rules and policies, was mailed out prior to school opening. In it parents were requested not to call teachers at their homes in the evenings or during weekends, since they don't deal with life-threatening situations that could not wait till the next school day. If the parents felt strongly about needing to speak to a teacher, immediately, they should call me at home and I would relay the message to the teacher. This rule was very much appreciated by entire faculty.

I have also convinced the school boards of the need to engage a social worker, a special ed. teacher, and two separate remedial teachers, one for each area of studies. The need for such a setup was amply demonstrated by the fact that some Jewish children could not benefit from a total experience of a good day school education, because of some learning and/or emotional problems that could be alleviated by these specially trained personnel. They became an integral part of the total school program. T.U. was so impressed with this new, and at that time nothing short of a revolutionary idea, that I was asked to write a special article describing the Special Needs program and all of the procedures that we had developed to identify the students that were at risk and in need of support services. The article was complete, exhaustive in all of its details and with its professional lexicon. It was published in *Hamenahel*, at first, soliciting input and opinions about it. Later it was printed by T.U. as a separate treatise and made available for purchase from T.U. Publications as offered in their catalog of books, workbooks, and pamphlets of interest to all educators and parents.

Many voluntary, extra-curricular programs, of recreational and enrichment value, for after-school hours, were offered free of charge. At the end of the first year, about ten to twelve different ninety-minute programs were going on with a large participation. They included science club, art club, ballet, Hebrew conversation club, chess club, Israeli dance club, orchestra, choir, etc. These became very popular. Within a year or two they were extended, by popular demand, to about fifteen such clubs.

As soon as Ms. Biddick was hired, she and I went down to the State Department of Education to see Mr. Hall, who was in charge of private school accreditations, to determine what it would take for me to become acceptable as principal and administrator of Hillel, within the regulations for such accreditation. He was extremely helpful. He looked over my transcripts from Herzliah Hebrew Teachers Institute and my letters of recommendations and decided that I have met the requirements for a B.A. equivalency in education. He issued me an official, regular Type A teacher's license, valid for five years, with an endorsement qualifying me to teach Hebrew language, philosophy, literature, and theology in any public school in the state of Colorado. Mr. Hall also wrote a letter of introduction to Prof. Nolte, the dean of the graduate school of Educational Administration, at the University of Denver, recommending that I be admitted as a "special student" to earn the required thirty-five credit points to receive a Type D, administrator's license from the State Department of Education.

Once again, Ms. Biddick came with me, as a "good mother" would, to the D.U. campus on registration day, to help me register for the needed classes. We stood in line for endless hours, shoulder to shoulder, with all the thousands of young students trying to fill out their registration cards and pick the classes they thought would be the easy ones to pass. Our turn finally came. We showed Dr. Nolte the letter from Mr. Hall and the Type A certificate, which meant that I earned the prerequisite B.A. degree in education. Ms. Biddick explained to Dr. Nolte that since I would be employed by a Hebrew day school, rather than by a public school, the fact that my teaching certificate is endorsed only for Hebrew related subjects should not concern the university. Dr. Nolte agreed. I was given a schedule of classes that met in the late afternoons and evenings, so that it would not interfere with my teaching and administrative duties. I would most likely have to forget about making plans for summer vacations, since to earn the needed credits in night school classes only, it would take a much longer time than the three years the university required for the completion of the entire program. My time was now completely spoken for. Running the school, teaching, going to the university in the evening and at night, preparing term papers, reading the required textbooks, studying for semi-finals and finals, plus meetings of all sorts, etc., kept me more than busy. Interestingly, the more the pressure piled up, the less "sick" I began to feel.

My contract was renewed for the next three years, as a full-time principal. My studies were hard, as were the admission tests to graduate school. I read English painfully slow, for while I was reading I was also studying the syntax of sentence structure and the spelling of words. Ms. Biddick found it hard to follow some of the things that we did differently at Hillel than at the public schools. I spent a lot of time trying to explain and to justify to her why I was making certain decisions. At the end of her second year at Hillel, she wrote to the board that she was confident that I am now "eager to work alone" and that I would do well running the school by myself.

Dr. Nolte followed my academic work very closely. He took a special interest in my progress. He asked me one day why I wanted to stop my studies after earning the required thirty-five credits. Why don't I continue to earn the required forty-five credits to earn a bona-fide master's degree in the field of Educational Administration? After some review of my grades (A's and only two B's), he decided to change my status from "special student" to "regular" graduate school candidate for the master's degree in Educational Administration.

While at Denver University I met, once again, with Mr. Hall of the State Department of Education. This time as a fellow student, earning credits toward the five-year compulsory renewal of his administrator's license. Hillel Academy of Denver became the first, fully accredited private school in the state of Colorado, on a voluntary rather than compulsory basis. Dr. Nolte brought the entire class of students from D.U. to hear me address the full house of State Representatives at the Capitol, representing the private and parochial schools of the state in the request for state support, in the form of vouchers for all students in non-public schools. I had previously done so "in chambers" of the Education Committee of the House of Representatives. Those events were reported both in the daily newspapers and in the Catholic and the Jewish weekly papers. I was truly riding a high crest of acceptability in my chosen profession.

In 1970, I actually graduated from D.U., after passing the final examinations, with a master of arts degree, with an emphasis on Educational Administration. Of course, I also received my Type D (Elementary School principal) license. Dr. Nolte tried to persuade me to stay on and work on a Ph.D. program on a full scholarship. I just could not do it. The school had grown in population to over 250 students and the staff grew to thirty-five full-time and some part-time individuals. This demanded my full attention. After trying one more year with an outside non-Jewish consultant, before I received my license, the board and I decided that there was no longer any compelling reason to have my duties shared with anyone else. I was now in total charge of the entire running of the school, solo. No assistants, helpers or coordinators of any kind.

The yearly T.U. principals' conventions at the Pioneer Country Club in the New York Catskill Mountains were always a high point for both Tova and me. We usually made a full week's vacation of it, staying in a good hotel in Manhattan (on 5th Avenue and 55th Street), eating in good restaurants and then, on Wednesday, we would get a ride out to the mountains until Sunday noon. Without fail, at every such convention and at regional conferences of T.U., I was always on the program, delivering at least one or two lectures on some educational topics, or explaining some innovative and exciting programs that we were trying out at Hillel. Many of my lectures were also printed in T.U. publications. Life was great. There was much to be happy about.

Both David and Meir each celebrated their becoming a Bar Mitzvah in a most modest fashion. No invitations were printed or sent out to anyone. The entire community was invited to an open-house reception on the Sunday, following each Bar Mitzvah. In keeping with my own experience, when I became a Bar Mitzvah, and true to my own philosophy that much too much pressure is put on the boys to "perform," each one trying to outdo the next one in some sort of a contest of who was the better performer, we decided not to teach them the reading of the Torah or to daven as a *shaliach tzibur*. Neither of them expressed any desire to do so. They each were just called up to the Torah (Meir also recited the Haftarah). We had no catered affairs and no gathering of the clan to help with the festivities.

My contract was renewed every three years, with nice increments. I was by now very secure in my position. In the words of Dr. Joseph Kaminetzky, the National Director of T.U., I had become "Mr. Day School." At one of the principals' conventions, I was completely surprised to be especially honored by being the first principal ever to be publicly presented with a beautiful citation "for meritorious achievement," the first of many awards and citations from various institutions. I was also appointed by the Colorado State Department of Education to serve a three-year term as a member of the Title I Advisory Committee. I was also asked by D.U. to deliver several lectures on the Holocaust to various groups of students.

The annual fundraising banquets of the school were great events. Dressed in my own tuxedo, I delivered speeches in front of several hundreds of guests. Ironically, speech-making, writing advertisements, promotional and various enrollment materials, the very aspects of the principal-ship which I feared the most at first, became some of my favorite activities. I spoke at Bar Mitzvah celebrations as well as on other occasions.

Letters of recognition and praise for my work poured in from many directions. Aside from the usual problems of dealing with irate mothers, "prima donna" staff members, spoiled and pampered children, obstinate board members, etc., I really enjoyed being at the hub and at the center of events. I was always prepared with data and answers for all board and committee meetings. Things could not have possibly been better for us. I had security, fairly good health, fame and self-assurance, or so I thought.

EPILOGUE

Some of these flashback scenes, memories, sketches, fears, and terrors of my past history and how I came to be in the position and in the predicament in which I am now, come racing through my aching head in a helter-skelter and random sequences, as I am waiting in that cold hallway for word about x's condition.

Finally, her parents arrive, with shock and deep worry registered on their faces. I fill them in on the details of the accident. Slowly I start to calm down. Instead of them blaming me for the accident, they actually reassure me that there is no reason for me to be so shaken. I am relieved.

Together we wait until the doctor comes out to report that their little girl will be okay. They had to sew up her arm with eighty-five stitches! It takes a long time to reconnect all the severed arteries and veins. A plastic surgeon is called to help minimize the appearance of the large scar that would form after the cut would heal.

POSTSCRIPT

I continued to serve Hillel Academy as its principal until 1983. After three additional years as principal of the day school in Hartford, Connecticut, we moved to Israel on a trial basis. After a three-week lecture tour in Johannesburg, South Africa, as an emissary of the Jewish Agency Department of Torah Education, we decided to come back to Denver.

There is a very interesting story to tell as to the reasons why we decided to leave Hillel Academy after serving the community faithfully for twenty-five years, and wander around from place to place. But that story will have to wait for now and perhaps will someday be written as a sequel to this story.

My life from Chust to Auschwitz to New York to Denver to Hartford to Israel to South Africa and back to Denver tells the story of the resilience of the human spirit and what can be achieved with positive values and constructive goals as your guides.

The "tattooed" principal has persevered and triumphed over most of his persecutors. Albeit, the price paid was enormous, and in spite of the ghosts and demons of the horrors of the past come piercing through the very fragile facade put up with such great efforts, to temporarily paralyze the creative energies during the day, and to terrorize the tranquility of the night with horrific nightmares of the past... in spite of our tormentors, we continue to live, to be creative, and to contribute to the societies that are willing to accept us as equals.

Family L to R: Israel
Rosenfeld, Mother
Chanah Rosenfeld,
brother Yoel Rosenfeld,
sister Leah Rosenfeld

Young Couple:
Israel and Tova
Rosenfeld

Army:
Israel (Izzy)
Rosenfeld
in the Army,
1951

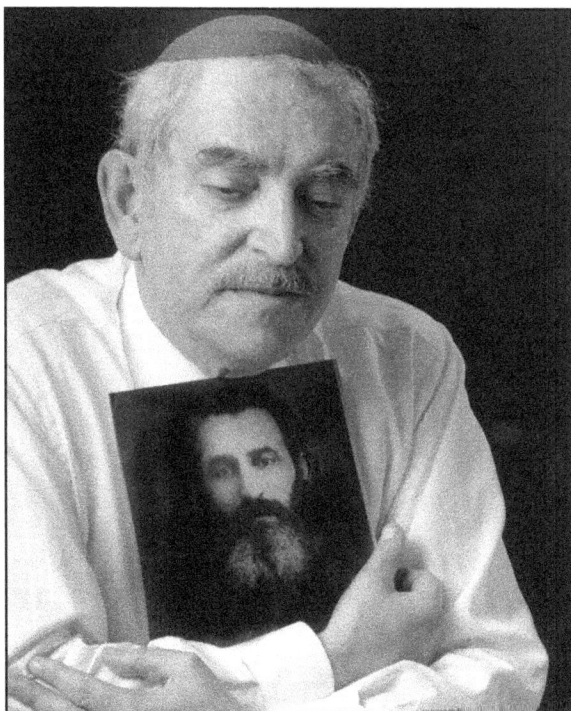

With Father: Rabbi Rosenfeld with picture
of his father, David Rosenfeld

With President: Rabbi Rosenfeld with
Israeli President Ephraim Katzir

Wedding: Israel and Tova Rosenfeld
wedding in Yerushalayim

Rosenfelds: Rabbi and Mrs. Rosenfeld

Rabbi Israel Rosenfeld

AFTERWORD
by Scott Friedman

The morning of January 26, 2015, the world as I've known it my entire life irrevocably changed. Rabbi Israel Rosenfeld passed away. Of course, I have known many other people in my lifetime whose time has passed. Some of these people have impacted my life in significant ways. But the change that I felt on that morning was unique. For me, and for so many others, Rabbi Rosenfeld was not just a person that I knew or an individual that impacted my life. He was an indispensable part of my understanding of the meaning of this world that G-d has created for us in which to dwell.

As the reader knows from the pages of this book, Rabbi Rosenfeld spent the majority of his life in Denver, Colorado. What is difficult to glean, however, from Rabbi Rosenfeld's modest words, is the extent of the impact that he had on the Denver Jewish community and the rest of *klal Yisrael*. When you speak with anyone that knew him, you are sure to hear about his effervescent smile, his ability to make you feel as if you were the only person in the world that mattered and his passion for Jewish education. Former students will surely impart stories of Rabbi Rosenfeld correcting their *dikduk* (Hebrew grammar), checking to see if they were wearing their *tzitzit* (traditional ceremonial garment worn by Jewish males), and applying firm yet compassionate discipline.

But the essence of Rabbi Rosenfeld lay further beneath the surface. He was a man that lived two lives. Although in many

242

ways they were separate and distinct from each other, in other ways they were inextricably tied. Rabbi Rosenfeld did not shy away from his past as a survivor of Auschwitz and the Holocaust. He regularly shared his story with students, friends, and strangers alike. But as many have shared in the days since Rabbi Rosenfeld's passing, when you finished the conversation with him you did not walk away feeling hopeless and in despair. None of us that did not experience the Holocaust can possibly begin to imagine the impact it had on those that fell victim to its evil. There have been many well documented reactions from survivors from the likes of Viktor Frankl, Primo Levi and Eli Wiesel, to name a few. Some, like Frankl, were able to find meaning in the world despite the atrocities that they experienced. Others, like Levi, seemed to have never really left the brutality of the concentration camps.

What stood out about Rabbi Rosenfeld is that he left Auschwitz with a faith in G-d and a determination to not only a personal commitment to his faith, but a commitment to spread that faith to the next generations of Jewish children. As a school child learning about the Holocaust, it was difficult for me to understand what lessons to take away from the subject. The common question of how it was possible for G-d to let this happen to his people was forefront in my mind. Was this evidence that G-d did not exist or that the Jewish people had no different relationship to Him than any other? But then there was Rabbi Rosenfeld, a survivor who walked in the valley of death and climbed up to the top of the mountain of life. To listen to him teach the words of the Gemara or to explain the meaning of the weekly *parashah* was to remove any doubt about the truth of the Jewish faith. He who had faced the ultimate test of faith was there to reassure us that the path of the Torah was the correct path upon which to travel.

This was the Rabbi Rosenfeld that I and so many others knew. A messenger from the heavens to help make sense of the world. If he could keep his faith after what he lived through, what possible challenges could prevent the rest of us from doing the same? But Rabbi Rosenfeld did not stop at reassuring those of strong Jewish faith that they should continue on in their Jewish lives. His commitment went well beyond that.

As the principal of Hillel Academy, Rabbi Rosenfeld created an environment that while it adhered to strict standards of *halachah* (Jewish law), it was an environment that was welcoming to Jewish children of all backgrounds. My own home as a child was not one with religious observance. However, my parents were not very excited about the local public schools, and at the suggestion of a business acquaintance they decided to set up a visit at Hillel Academy. Rabbi Rosenfeld greeted my parents with his typical kindness. As he toured them around the school, he shared his educational philosophy which included a strong Judaic education as well as a strong, well-rounded secular education. He assured my parents that my sister and I would not be looked down upon due to our background and that we would come out of school with the benefit of a true understanding of our heritage. My parents decided to enroll us.

Amongst both of my parents' siblings, there were ten children of my generation. Of those ten, only two—my sister and me— have Jewish children today. Between us we have fifteen children that were born into households that observe the commandments that G-d passed down to the Jewish people at Mount Sinai. Had it not been for Rabbi Rosenfeld and the environment that he created at Hillel Academy, my parents would never have felt comfortable sending my sister and me to an Orthodox Jewish day school. These children, and many others like them, are the true legacy of Rabbi Rosenfeld. Though the Nazis tried to wipe the Jewish people off of the face of the Earth, Rabbi Rosenfeld refused to go. And not only did he raise a wonderful family of his own with sons and grandchildren that have become Rabbis and educators in their own right, but he left behind an army of young Jews to carry on the faith and the mission that G-d set out for the Jewish people. These are the B'nai Yisrael, the children of Yisrael Rosenfeld.

www.ingramcontent.com/pod-product-compliance
Lightning Source LLC
Chambersburg PA
CBHW021357090426
42742CB00009B/891